The Complete Book of Surf Fishing

The Complete Book of Surf Fishing

AL RISTORI

Skyhorse Publishing

Skyhorse Publishing books may be purchased in bulk at special discounts for sales promotion, corporate gifts, fund-raising, or educational purposes. Special editions can also be created to specifications. For details, contact the Special Sales Department, Skyhorse Publishing, 555 Eighth Avenue, Suite 903, New York, NY 10018 or info@skyhorsepublishing.com.

www.skyhorsepublishing.com

Photos by Al Ristori
Additional photography copyright © Alberto Knie and copyright © Joe Blaze, except where otherwise credited.

10 9 8 7 6 5 4 3 2

Library of Congress Cataloging-in-Publication Data

Ristori, Al.
The complete book of surf fishing / Al Ristori.
p. cm.
ISBN-13: 978-1-60239-247-2 (pbk. : alk. paper)
ISBN-10: 1-60239-247-1 (pbk. : alk. paper) 1. Surf fishing. 2. Surf casting. I. Title.

SH457.2.R57 2008
799.16–dc22
2007042892

Printed in China

*To Joe Blaze, without whose help in photography,
downloading and conversion of my old slides to a digital format
this book never would have been completed.*

Contents

Introduction

Anglers who fish from the shore are a different breed. As difficult as it often is to catch fish from a boat, being restricted to a relatively small area and having to cast just to reach fishable water is a big disadvantage. It always amazes me when I'm successful, especially on those red-letter days when fish are stacked up in front of me and the fishing is actually better than could ordinarily be expected from a boat.

Indeed, the completion of this book was delayed by a call that bluefish had been blitzing the beach. I'd been boat fishing earlier in the day with Capt. Terry Sullivan, casting small plugs for mostly small striped bass in New Jersey's Navesink River (the original source of West Coast stripers) and cursing the big bluefish that were eating those plugs while interfering with our striper quest. Yet, bluefish in the surf are something else altogether—and I raced to the beach in hopes they might still be there.

A few birds were working offshore of Manasquan, along the northern New Jersey Shore, and I raced to the surf in front of them even though they were out of range. Since I'd forgotten to grab my pliers or a de-hooker, I decided for safety's sake to fish only with the single hook lures I'd thrown into the chest pocket of my waders. The first cast with a 2-ounce

Joe Brooks, as fishing editor for Outdoor Life *introduced a generation of anglers to the joys of surfcasting. (courtesy IGFA)*

diamond jig resulted in a hook–up with an 8-pound blue, and so did every other cast until the single hook broke as I was removing it from a bigger blue for another release. The two Tsunami shads I next utilized were sacrifices to the toothy critters, but they produced a few more blues and even a 23-inch striper that hit alongside a jetty. That left me only with a large Yo-Zuri Surface Cruiser that's a favorite lure though I didn't want to deal with the big treble hooks without pliers. Yet, every cast that late afternoon raised a bluefish from 7 to 13 pounds, and I was lucky enough to be able to remove them safely before one engulfed it and I had to conclude the evening by walking off the beach with that 12-pounder for the next

Surf fishing is a solitary pursuit. The angler, a seemingly endless shoreline, and the cycles of nature must come together for success. (Alberto Knie photo)

night's dinner. Thirteen large bluefish in less than an hour, and without having to move more than a few yards, is good fishing anywhere, and quite possible if you're in the surf at the right time.

A fisherman who expects that to happen on a regular basis is bound to be a disappointed angler. Those of us dedicated to the sport put in countless hours trying to be "at the right place at the right time," but only put it all together occasionally. Yet, there's a very special feeling of accomplishment when we do so. Even though I spend much of my time running a charter boat, I fish the surf as often as possible and have to agree with those who work the beach exclusively that "one fish from the surf is worth ten from a boat!"

My fascination with the surf started over a half-century ago when Mr. Kern, a kindly neighbor in Merrick, Long Island, took me to Jones Beach one Saturday morning to fish bloodworms in the surf. Though I didn't actually catch anything, a striped bass that was probably short of even the 16-inch minimum in effect at that time flipped off the hook in the wash before I could get to it. The bass got unhooked, but I was "hooked" on the surf.

Mr. Kern had real conventional (revolving spool) surfcasting tackle and could cast pretty well. It was another story when Billy McGuiness and I tried surfcasting on our own. We had started fishing by bicycling to Camman's Pond with bamboo poles to catch stunted sunfish. Our non-fishing fathers eventually bought us rods and reels, but they were short, stout boat outfits unsuited for casting even by an expert. We'd join my mother on her trips to Jones Beach for sunbathing and walk to the surf-fishing area where we waded out as far as possible in bathing suits before casting a sinker and baited hook, probably no more than 20 feet. Every cast with the revolving spool reels produced a backlash that we picked out while walking back to the beach.

Fortunately, there were a lot of blowfish and some northern kingfish in the surf those days, and we actually managed to catch an occasional fish, a thrill at any size for grammar school kids. Anything larger than a pound was unheard of for us though we'd heard that experienced fishermen caught much larger fish such as striped bass at night. I did beach a "sea monster," a 10-pound skate, while fishing one morning with Mr. Kern. That was by far my largest fish, and I remember proudly showing pictures of the ugly skate to my friends during eighth grade graduation from St. Barnabus in Bellmore.

Eventually, another neighbor built me a real 9-foot bamboo surf rod with just two guides and a Penn reel held on with clamps. My casts went a bit farther, but the backlashes became even larger.

It wasn't until spinning tackle became more common that my surf-casting significantly improved. What a difference there is now when a youngster can get started casting with an inexpensive spinning outfit and achieve success right away with relatively foolproof gear!

To be able to throw bait out into waters that all looked the same and actually catch something proved fascinating to this youngster, and I've never lost that awe even after learning more about cuts, sloughs and other

Rocky shorelines or expansive beaches, where the sea meets the shore is the realm of the surfcaster. Striped bass are the trophy quest in the northeast United States. (Charlie Fornabio photo)

Jetty rocks adjacent to the deep water of shipping channels are time honored producers for surf fishermen. (Joe Blaze photo)

This surfcaster briefly shares his water with a migrating whale.

aspects of the surf we knew nothing about at the time. It was a very simple experience in those days; just cast as far as possible over the first breaker!

Artificial lures weren't even a consideration then, as striped bass were unavailable when we could surf cast in the summer—and there were virtually no adult bluefish, even for boaters, at that time.

The first fish I caught casting a lure from a beach came years later after Naval Officer Candidate School, when I was transferred from a destroyer to serve as War Plans Officer at the United States Naval Station in Trinidad, in the West Indies. The base dentist and I bought a pirogue cut from a tree by local craftsmen and powered by a 12-horsepower West Bend outboard. For lack of any better place to keep it, we attached it to a mooring just off the beach at the Officer's Club, located on a cove off the open Caribbean. I had to swim out to the boat to use it, and one morning I walked down to the beach with my gear and saw a school of jack crevalle pushing bait into the wash. I had a spinning reel by that time and managed to get a metal lure out to the boiling jacks in time to catch one from shore.

My real introduction to lure fishing in the surf came after being discharged during the Cuban Crises. I passed up an opportunity to join the

An angler plies the surf as birds work the schools of bait at the end of the day. (Joe Blaze photo)

CIA in order to take a dream job for an angler, a sales position with the Harry C. Miller Co. manufacturer's representative for the Garcia Corporation. It was my good fortune to land a job selling the most popular fishing tackle in the country at the time, and during trips to New England I was able to learn about casting lures with such legends as wooden-lure craftsman Stan Gibbs, and Bob Pond of Atom Lures fame.

Most of my casting was still done from boats, but what I'd learned was put to good use from shore whenever possible, both there and at Montauk on the east end of Long Island. During the last few decades I've been living in New Jersey and doing most of my surfcasting there, though there have also been trips to North Carolina's Outer Banks and Florida's central eastern coast, plus such foreign areas as Ecuador, Panama, Costa Rica, and Australia. Wherever there's a shore I can get to for casting, I'll be giving it a try.

Strictly speaking, surf implies ocean swell breaking on a beach. Yet, the scope of this book is much broader. The angler casting in Cape Cod Canal considers himself a surfcaster even though there's no swell and he may not even need waders. Other "surfcasters" fish from the shores of large bays where the only waves are wind-driven rather than the result of swells, and they too will be represented here.

That also applies to those rugged anglers in South Africa, Hawaii, Japan, Korea, and other areas throughout the world who seize their opportunity to fish from shore while perched on rocks well above the sea and only get wet from the spray when a large swell crashes below them.

CHAPTER 1

The Development of Surfcasting

It's unlikely there's any record of when man first started surfcasting, but it probably began soon after line and hooks were developed. Those, plus a weight of some sort and bait, are basically all that's required to catch a fish from the surf. Tie on a stone for weight, twirl the rig above your head to gain momentum, and let it go at the right moment to send the crude rig to sea. Though very basic, that would prove effective even today when fish are within range. Merely wrapping the running line around a bottle or similarly shaped smooth object would improve casting performance. Indeed, it's not unusual to see shore fishermen in tropical areas use an inexpensive large plastic spool (sometimes referred to as a Cuban spinning reel) to accomplish such handline casts quite efficiently and for considerable distances.

Finely machined baitcasting reels revolutionized freshwater fishing long before spinning reels came along, and the same principles were incorporated into larger revolving spool reels for the surf. While an educated thumb could produce a decent cast with most conventional reels, those especially crafted for casting, such as the Penn Squidder, provided much more control and made it easier to avoid backlashes. Though the Squidder wasn't really very expensive, it was what surfcasters of the era when I was growing up aspired to own.

Hal Lyman plays out the end of the day in the classic surf of North Carolina in 1970. (Joel Arrington photo, courtesy IGFA)

Joe Brooks, Fishing Editor for Outdoor Life *and Frank Woolner, founder of* Salt Water Sportsman, *team up to land Brooks' striper in the Massachusetts surf. (Dick Woolner photo, courtesy IGFA)*

As noted in the introduction, spinning tackle has revolutionized the sport of surfcasting. It's no longer necessary to go through the rigors of learning to control a revolving spool reel while reaching for the horizon. Any beginner can go to a coastal tackle shop and be outfitted with a spinning rig that will permit him or her to cast adequately in most cases and have a good chance at immediate success rather than struggling through years of merely learning to cast well.

Red drum are a perennial favorite of surf anglers throughout their range. (courtesy IGFA)

It's not only the reels that make casting so much easier these days. Rods advanced from heavy bamboo, which often developed a set, to fiberglass and then even lighter and more powerful graphite. I started with linen line that not only broke easily, but also had to be washed and dried after every use in saltwater. Anglers had rollers set up in their basement so the linen could be taken off the reel each night and dried after being washed in fresh water. Then the synthetic braided lines, that didn't require any such care, came along, but nylon braid had too much stretch. Next was Dacron, a DuPont development that eliminated most of the stretch, but was hot under the thumb during the cast. Monofilament lines came in with spinning, but at first they were quite stiff, had little abrasion resistance, and weren't used on conventional reels because they were too springy and difficult to control, with even the "most educated thumb." I well remember putting mono on my first small spinning reel, a Ny-O-Lite nylon model my father figured would be best for saltwater. Not knowing anything about twist, I tried to reel on the mono as I did with braided lines and ended up

The tackle and gear may have changed over the years, but the appeal of surf fishing—the angler, the elements, and the life in the surf—still works the same magic. Note bluefish blasting bait over author's shoulder. (Joe Blaze photo)

with a mass of coiled-up line that had to be straightened out foot-by-foot in order to get it on the spool.

Not only are modern monofilaments supple and relatively abrasion-resistant, but we also have a new breed of tightly braided line that provides huge capacity on relatively small reels while delivering greater line test in a tiny diameter. The crack of line snapping whenever we used to make a hard cast that resulted in a backlash has become almost a memory with the new braids and spinning tackle. Instead of going through several sinkers a day, we now often retire the same sinker we set out with after the season is over.

Many pros stayed with conventional reels long after spinning became readily available at reasonable prices because they were more reliable and had better drags for fighting large fish. That's not generally the case any longer as there are spinners available that have both the capacity and drag with which to battle the greatest game fish. The Shimano Stella I use for casting to big stripers is the same reel I've cast from a center console in Panama to boat a 170-pound yellowfin tuna fish far more powerful and much faster than anything likely to ever be encountered in the surf.

The theory of surfcasting remains constant over the decades: Find the bait and imitate it wisely for success. This bluefish hit a surface lure while feeding on baby menhaden (peanut bunkers).

Everything about surfcasting has been improved over the last few decades, in addition to lighter, more efficient tackle. When I started, almost everyone fished in hip boots, rushing down to the surf for the cast and running back before a crashing wave got their pants wet. Now most surfcasters in cool water areas wear waders that provide more complete protection and even come in lightweight, breathable versions that make walking the beach a pleasure.

CHAPTER 2

The Surfcaster's Favorite Species

Not all fish come within range of surfcasters, but most do at one time or another. As will be discussed in Chapter 12, there are even occasions when bluefin and yellowfin tuna can be caught by intrepid anglers casting from rocks along the South African coast, and the oddball oceanic fish will blunder near the surf under very rare circumstances. However, those game fish listed here are among the most sought after by surfcasters. World records listed are International Game Fish Association (IGFA) all-tackle records as of 2007.

STRIPED BASS (*Morone saxatilis*)

The most popular inshore migratory species of the United States Atlantic coast ranges from North Carolina to Maine, and into the Canadian Maritime Provinces. Isolated river populations exist farther south along the coast and even into the Gulf of Mexico. The landlocked population of the Santee-Cooper Reservoir system has been transplanted throughout much of the United States to stock freshwater lakes across the country. Striped bass from New Jersey's Navesink River were transported by rail after the transcontinental railroad was completed, and from that stocking the species established itself on the West Coast from the San Francisco area (where they provide surfcasting opportunities) up to Oregon.

Striped bass are one of the premier game fish in the northeast surf, and just because the sun goes down is no reason to pack up and leave. This one was taken at night by famed Montauk surfcaster "Crazy Alberto" Knie. (Alberto Knie photo)

Stripers are anadromous fish living in saltwater, but spawning in rivers. The major population spawns in the Chesapeake Bay river system (where they're called rock, or rockfish), but the Delaware and Hudson rivers are also important spawning areas. Though they can live almost anywhere, stripers require long rivers for successful spawning and only a few river systems meet that requirement.

This long-living and fast-growing species is clearly identified by the 7 to 8 black stripes along the sides. Though the vast majority of trophy stripers are taken from boats, a great many are available to surfcasters. Indeed, the IGFA world record is a 78-pounder caught by Albert McReynolds

Striped bass, like this "short" one about to be released by the author at Sea Girt New Jersey, are the mainstay of surfcasters in the Northeast. (Joe Blaze photo)

from an Atlantic City, New Jersey, jetty at night during a northeast storm on September 21, 1982. There are records of stripers taken commercially centuries ago that weighed as much as 125 pounds.

Anglers catch mostly school stripers from a few pounds up to the minimum size (currently 28 inches along the East Coast), as well as many 20- to 30-pounders. A 50-pounder is the dream of every striper addict, and many experts fish a lifetime without catching one.

Striped bass are the ideal surf fish, as they respond readily to a wide variety of lures and baits, are good-eating, and fight well. The only thing they don't do is jump, but they often provide impressive surface strikes on poppers and swimmers. This was the species that attracted many anglers to the surf after WWII and led to the development of modern saltwater plugs and the extensive use of beach buggies.

Prime surfcasting areas include Cape Cod, Martha's Vineyard, and Nantucket, Massachusetts; Watch Hill, Charlestown Breachway, and Block Island, Rhode Island; Montauk, New York; Sandy Hook, Island Beach State Park, and Barnegat Light, New Jersey; plus Hatteras, North Carolina, in the winter.

BLUEFISH (*Pomatomus salatrix*)

Often encountered by northeast Atlantic coast surfcasters at the same time striped bass are feeding on the same bait fish, blues aren't nearly as appreciated due to their sharp teeth and darker flesh that isn't desirable to those who don't like "fishy" fish. They are great game fish by any standard, being strong fighters that often jump when hooked. Lures are frequently cut off by those "choppers," and wood plugs that will last for years when only hit by stripers are chewed up by blues. These were traditionally cyclical fish, going through periods of great abundance and then almost disappearing. However, the current cycle has been going on since the 1950s and shows no signs of diminishing, especially in the prime area of New York Bight.

Blues range from Florida to Maine along the Atlantic coast, and are also found in lesser quantities in the Gulf of Mexico, where they are generally smaller. The same species is also found in many temperate and tropical waters throughout the world, but not in the eastern Pacific. I've caught them in such widely separated areas as Trinidad in the Caribbean and South Africa. Most blues range from a few pounds up to 15 pounds, with a

Bluefish are regular and dependable as they migrate spring and fall along much of the Northeast Coast. Allen Riley removes his lure carefully in order to avoid the sharp teeth. (Allen Riley photo)

few exceeding 20 pounds. The world record is a 31-pounder trolled by James M. Hussey in Hatteras Inlet, North Carolina, on January 30, 1972.

WEAKFISH (*Cynoscion regalis*)

The third of the northeast Atlantic coast Big Three for surfcasters is so-named because of its soft mouth that frequently results in pulled hooks. It has been the most cyclical of fish, ranging from great abundance to almost complete elimination over the years. Those swings haven't been as pronounced since management by the Atlantic States Marine Fisheries Commission (ASMFC) started. Weakfish resemble trout, and are often referred to as sea trout in the south and gray trout in the Chesapeake. The closely related spotted sea trout (*Cynoscion nebulosus*) is the number-one saltwater recreational fishing catch in numbers, but is mostly taken in bays and rivers. There are plenty of shore fishing opportunities inside inlets, and some are taken from the Hatteras surf during cold weather.

Spawning weakfish, often exceeding 10 pounds, enter bays from the Chesapeake to Rhode Island's Narragansett (where they're referred to by the Indian name *squeteague*) in the spring, though they aren't often encountered in the surf at that time. Shore casters do get into those trophy weaks (that can reach 20 pounds or more) from the shores of rivers and bays by casting jigs and flies. Surfcasters catch weakfish in the summer, and especially during the migration to the south during the fall. The mostly 1- to 5-pound weaks rarely hit popping plugs, but readily attack small swimming plugs, jigs, flies, and metal lures as well as a wide variety of baits. They are white-meated fish, but rather soft, and don't freeze well.

RED DRUM (*Sciaenops ocellatus*)

The most-desired surf fish along North Carolina's Outer Banks grows to great sizes. The IGFA world record of 94⅛ pounds was taken on November 7, 1984, from the surf at Avon by Dave Deuel, a young marine biologist for the National Marine Fisheries Service. The one or more black spots on the base of the tail are a sure identification mark on the copper-colored body. Red drum in the surf are caught primarily on bait, and night is the prime time. Anglers often line up virtually shoulder-to-shoulder at Hatteras when the run of 30- to 50-pounders is on. In the rare instances

Weakfish, known for their soft mouths, are a popular target along the East Coast for surfcasters such as "Crazy Alberto" Knie. (Alberto Knie photo)

when they are spotted swimming, red drum will hit lures such as spoons and other metals. This species used to be known as channel bass, and was common as far north as Barnegat Inlet, New Jersey, but is rarely encountered there any longer. There's also a surf fishery for smaller red drum, usually referred to as puppy drum and highly desired as food fish. Red

Red drum, identified by the black tail spot, willingly take a range of artificial and natural baits. Locally called redfish in Florida, they are great game fish and fine table fare at this size, when they're commonly referred to as puppy drum. (Joe Blaze photo)

drum are abundant in the Gulf of Mexico, though surfcasting for them isn't as important there.

SNOOK (*Centropomus undecimalis*)

This great food and game fish frequents the Florida surf during the fall mullet run, though it's also a prime target of shore casters inside the inlets at other times. Snook are also common in the Central American surf at river mouths from late summer into the fall. The world record of 53 pounds, 10 ounces, was taken by Gilbert Ponzi at Parismina, Costa Rica, on October 18, 1978. The almost identical black snook (*Centropomus nigrescens*) of the Pacific also frequents similar areas, and is taken on a variety of plugs, jigs and flies. The IGFA record of 57 pounds, 12 ounces, was taken by George Beck

Snook such as this one that hit the author's swimming plug at night in the Parismina River, Costa Rica, prowl the southern climes. Snook are a prime target for Florida surfcasters.

on August 23, 1991, at Rio Naranjo, Costa Rica. I've caught them in that country as well as Panama and the Galapagos Islands.

TARPON (*Megalops atlanticus*)

The silver king is an occasional visitor to the Atlantic and Caribbean surf. As noted in Chapter 7, they are available along Florida's eastern coast during the fall mullet run. They can also be spotted rolling off Gulf of Mexico beaches at times, but are often difficult to tempt in that generally flat surf. As will be detailed in Chapter 12, tarpon provide great shore fishing opportunities along Central America's Caribbean coast around river mouths. Tarpon found in the surf are usually larger fish, from 50 pounds up to well over 100 pounds, and they'll hit a wide variety of lures. Virtually all tarpon are released. The world record 283-pounders were caught in Venezuela and Sierra Leone.

CREVALLE JACK (*Caranx hippos*)

This great fighting fish of the tropical Atlantic isn't generally desired as food, but it will tie up the angler for considerable periods of time before giving in. They range from 2-pounders up to well over 20 pounds and can grow to about 60 pounds. They frequently move into the Florida surf on both sides of the peninsula. The almost identical Pacific jack crevalle (*Caranx caninus*) is a common visitor to the surf.

ROOSTERFISH (*Nematistius pectoralis*)

Perhaps the greatest inshore game fish of the tropical eastern Pacific, and certainly the most beautiful. The world record is a huge 114-pounder caught by Abe Sackheim at La Paz, Baja California, Mexico, on June 1, 1960. Most roosterfish run from 15 to 50 pounds, and they're usually unable to resist live baits. On the other hand, it's a real challenge to catch them on lures that must be moved at high speed to fool them. Popping plugs and chuggers work well at times, though you're likely to get more follows than hook-ups. Even that is exciting as the coxcomb dorsal fin tantalizingly weaves behind the plug right up to the beach. Roosterfish patrol sandy shores as well as rocky areas, and often visit the surf, particularly at dawn. Indeed, boat fishermen cast lures as far as possible toward the beach when seeking roosterfish. They're

Tarpon migrate and feed along the surfline in the southern United States and tropical Central America, presenting a big-game target for shorebound anglers. The author plugged this one at the mouth on the Parismina river in Costa Rica.

Jack crevalle are heavyweight brawlers in the surf, hitting a variety of lures and baits.

common from Baja California to Ecuador, and California surfcasters have found good concentrations along the Pacific coast near Cabo San Lucas.

THE TUNAS

While bluefin and yellowfin tuna are rarely available to surfcasters, some have been caught from the rocks in South Africa and other areas which deep oceanic waters run close to shore. In addition, a few have been landed

Roosterfish, such as this one hooked on an A.O.K. lure, present an exotic challenge for anglers in the warm waters of the Pacific.

by fortunate surfcasters from beaches on Long Island during those rare years when blue waters move far inshore in the summer. Yet, there is one tuna that is both common and highly desired in the surf.

Though the little tunny (*Euthynnus alletteratus*) is the poorest eating fish in the tuna tribe, it fights just as hard as the others and is primarily a coastal species. It's most common from the Gulf of Mexico and along the Atlantic coast up to Cape Cod. As a surf fish, it is sought primarily from New Jersey to the Massachusetts islands. Anglers only get brief late-summer to early-fall shots at little tunny, and try to fool those sharp-eyed

Angler with a little tunny caught at dawn. (Joe Blaze photo)

tunas with small metal or lead-head jigs retrieved at high speed. They respond especially well to flies when fly-fishermen are able to get casts to them. Little tunny quite frequently feed on tiny bait, making it very difficult to fool them with lures. As with other tunas, they make long high-speed runs, and are great game fish. Anglers specializing in catching them often tie lures directly to mono, rather than using leaders, and take their chances of being cut off by bluefish that are usually common at the same time. The average size of those caught in the surf is about 6 to 12 pounds.

Little tunny are readily identified by several small black spots under their pectoral fins plus mackerel-like markings on their backs. They are invariably referred to in the southern Atlantic and the Gulf of Mexico as *bonita*, a name that confuses them with another branch of the family—the Atlantic bonito (*Sarda sarda*).

Nick Honachesky shows off a bonito caught on Crippled Herring lure at Bay Head, New Jersey.

In northern portions of the Atlantic coast, the common name is false alba-core, which confuses them with the albacore (*Thunnus alalunga*) that shares the typical tuna shape, but is a deepwater species distinguished by its long pectoral fins. Furthermore, the albacore provides premium canned tuna, whereas the little tunny must be soaked in milk or brine to remove all blood in order to make it edible. Thus, virtually all little tunny caught by surfcasters are released after an exciting battle. Those fish fight so hard that when releasing them it's often necessary to work them back and forth in the water while holding the tail before they're ready to dart away. The little tunny is replaced in the Pacific by two very similar-looking species, the black skipjack (*Euthynnus lineatus*) and the kawakawa (*Euthynnus affinis*).

The Atlantic bonito, as well as related species in the Pacific, is distin-guished by the stripes on its back, but not on the belly. It's a fine-eating, white-meated fish that makes occasional forays into the surf, most com-monly from New Jersey to Martha's Vineyard.

The tuna tribe belongs to the *Scombridae* family, which includes the mackerels.

The Spanish mackerel (*Scomberomous maculatus*) occasionally ventures within range of surfcasters in the Mid-Atlantic states, but does so much

Spanish mackerel, upper left, joins a pompano and a bluefish for a de facto surf grand slam along the Florida coast.

more commonly in Florida. Distinguished by a slim, spotted body and a mouthful of small, sharp teeth, Spanish mackerel average only a pound or two and rarely achieve even 10 pounds. They can be fooled by the same fast retrieve with small metal or lead-head lures as used for little tunny, but cut-offs are common when wire leaders aren't used. The Pacific sierra mackerel (*Scomberomous sierra*) may also be hooked in the surf at times, and it is a larger species than the Spanish—sometimes exceeding 10 pounds.

BOTTOM FISH

Surfcasters have a much better chance of catching bottom fish than the mercurial game species. Most desired is the Florida pompano (*Trachinotus carolinus*), a golden-hued gourmet species that's caught by specialists using very long surf rods enabling them to cast over the outer bars along Florida's eastern coast.

Sand fleas are the favored bait. Most pompano weigh 1 to 3 pounds, but can reach 7 pounds or more. They will also hit small jigs at times, and

Three pompano caught on conventional surf tackle with English bait-style hooks in the Florida surf. Gourmet grade fare, pompano have inspired a virtual religion among anglers along the Southeast Coast.

This fluke came out of the surf at Sandy Hook, New Jersey. The author poses before releasing the fish, which is short of legal size. (Joe Blaze photo)

many of those caught on the North Carolina Outer Banks are taken in that fashion during the summer by anglers casting with light tackle as the pompano are close to the beach there.

The summer flounder (*Paralichthys dentatus*) is a target for Mid-Atlantic surfcasters as well as those casting from shores at, or inside, inlets. It's replaced farther south by the very similar southern flounder (*Paralichthys lethostigma*) that also grows to 20 pounds or so, but usually weighs only 1 to 3 pounds. Fluke is the name applied to the summer flounder from northern New Jersey to New England. From the southern end of New Jersey south it's usually just "flounder" since the winter flounder isn't common in that area. Fluke are active feeders caught primarily on baits moved along the bottom rather than just lying there. They'll hit lures of many types, with flies, lead-head jigs and metal being the likely choices. Tipping the jig with a plastic grub or a Gulp Swimming Mullet will improve your chances, as will running a teaser above the lure. Most fluke caught in the surf aren't even of current legal sizes, but some from 2 to 5 pounds are taken. "Doormats" of 10 pounds or more are very rare, though a fly-rod surfcaster caught one of that size at Sandy Hook, New Jersey, a few years ago when it hit right in the wash.

The Atlantic croaker (*Micropogonias undulates*) is a common bottom fish from Florida to New Jersey. A member of the drum family, it's a cyclical species often available in great quantities around Chesapeake and Delaware Bays. They'll hit a variety of cut baits, such as clams, squid, and seaworms, on small hooks. Surfcasting for these usually pound-size fish (that can grow to about 6 pounds, but rarely exceed 3 pounds) is most effective at dawn and dusk if the tide is right.

The northern kingfish (*Menticirrhus saxatilis*) is a small, colorful species of the Mid-Atlantic surf that was my target as a young surfcaster. Most weigh less than a pound, though they may grow to 3 or 4 pounds.

This beautiful fish is excellent table fare, and doesn't resemble other members of the drum family except for the almost identical species that replace it to the south, the southern and gulf kingfishes. Local names in the South include roundhead, sea mink, sea mullet and whiting, since kingfish is the common name there for the much different king mackerel. All kingfish are easily identified by a rounded snout, tiny mouth, and a short barbel on the chin.

The California corbina (*Menticirrhus undulates*) is the Pacific version of the kingfish, ranging from California to Peru. A very popular species with

Tony Arcabascio with a colorful northern kingfish caught casting from his dock in Bayville, New Jersey. This species was the author's "big game" in the surf as a youngster.

California surfcasters, it's also long been protected from commercial fishing. Small baits such as soft-shell crabs, seaworms, mussels, ghost shrimp, and clams are favored.

California surfcasters also catch a variety of surf perches from the family *Embiotocidae*. Most are less than a foot in length and hit the same baits used for corbina.

CHAPTER 3

Tackle

There's hardly any type of tackle that isn't used for shore fishing some-where. For instance, ultra-light spinning can be utilized in calm surf such as is often available along Florida's Gulf coast. I've even seen big game gear, incapable of being cast, in use on North Carolina's Outer Banks as well as off inlet jetties where anglers use currents and balloons to carry baits out to sharks. Even within the parameters of more normal casting tackle there's still a very wide variety favored in different areas under various circumstances.

BASIC CONSIDERATIONS IN ROD CONSTRUCTION

The concept of rod weight has been modified over the years due to the development of space age materials. The unwieldy bamboo surf rod I started with was both heavy and insensitive. It was a new world when I first used a 9-foot, 2-piece Garcia fiberglass spinning rod with a metal ferrule and agate guides. While that represented a huge improvement in weight, sensitivity and casting performance, it now seems primitive as graphite has become the standard rod-building material.

There are many types of graphite, but all of them, even the less-expensive graphite-fiberglass composites, are superior to those fiberglass models I was delighted with in the 1960s.

Al Ristori and Bob Correll are using flexible-tip spinning rods to help animate the popper lures they are using for bluefish. The blur and slight bend in Bob's rod indicates that he is using a moderate wrist action to make the popper "dance" during the retrieve. (Joe Blaze photo)

Another basic decision in rod selection involves choosing a 1-piece or 2-piece rod. There's no questioning that 1-piece rods are preferable. If you can transport and store long, 1-piece rods, that should be your choice. However, if that's a problem, you'll find plenty of very good 2-piece models that will do the job. The development of internal ferrules to connect the two pieces has made all the difference in casting characteristics and dependability as breakage at metal ferrules used to be common whereas modern internal ferrules flex with the rod.

While those old agate guides protected the line from fraying, they were also subject to cracking, after which the sharp edge of the crack would quickly ruin the line. The development of aluminum oxide and other space-age guide materials has eliminated that worry. Now we can fish for years with the same guides that require no maintenance other than a spray of fresh water.

Fly and spin anglers share a jetty. (Joe Blaze photo)

Cork and synthetic materials are the usual choices for handles and fore grip, but tape-wrapped handles are popular with many pros. They used to be available only in custom rods, but some manufacturers now offer such models that provide a surer grip.

Graphite reel seats have replaced metal in most cases and are more comfortable to use, especially in cold weather.

STANDARD SURF SPINNING

The tackle most commonly associated with surfcasting is a long rod, capable of lengthy casts, with a large spinning reel. In one form or another, that's the practical gear for reaching over waves and getting bait or lures out to, or beyond, the outer bar along most of the Atlantic and Pacific coasts. Yet, within that broad category, there's a large range of tackle usually dictated more by the conditions and terminal tackle rather than the size of the fish.

Pompano specialists along Florida's central east coast use very long and heavy rods to cast heavy sinkers as far as possible for fish that weigh

Spinning reels, such as this Team Daiwa Advantage, are standard tackle for lure fishing. This one has been paired with a custom rod using a Fisher blank from Betty & Nick's Tackle Shop, Seaside Park, New Jersey. Locally built rods with top of the line reels provide an outfit tailored to the demands of the angler's home waters. (Joe Blaze photo)

only a pound or two, while striper pros working Cape Cod's sand beaches may use much lighter rigs to cast relatively light lures for fish that might be 25 times larger, but are close to shore.

Thus, the first consideration in selecting surf tackle should be how you'll be fishing rather than how big the fish may be. A rod suitable for heaving heavy sinkers and bait will be more of an ordeal when used for casting lures than it would be if it were simply being set in a sand spike after the cast is made.

Comfort is a prime factor when casting lures, and it's better to go light than to be prepared for a huge fish that may never be encountered. The only way you're going to catch fish with lures is to constantly cast and

These pompano were taken on sand fleas rigged with a float to hold the bait off the bottom to avoid crabs. A small pyramid sinker anchors the rig to the sandy bottom where pompano feed.

retrieve. Heavy tackle that quickly wears you out works against this most important factor and also limits the range of lures that can be utilized. Though some rods may be versatile enough to be passable for casting lures and still have enough backbone for casting heavy sinkers, you'll soon come to the realization that if you're spending very much time fishing both ways you'll need two very different rigs to fish comfortably and efficiently.

Not only are heavy rods a problem, but so too are large reels. The availability of the new braided lines has made it possible to use smaller reels that still pack more than enough high-break-strength line to handle anything likely to be encountered in the surf short of a huge shark.

In normal ocean surf situations, a 9- to 10-foot medium-action rod in combination with an intermediate-size spinning reel holding about 200 yards of 50-pound braid plus some backing should be relatively comfortable to cast with while still being capable of stopping any fish sought. Keep in mind the fact that this is the most general of recommendations as local circumstances plus your own physical capabilities will determine what's best to use. The only absolute requirement is that the rig be balanced. It's most likely that whatever you select as a first surfcasting rod won't be your last!

Pompano fishermen in Florida place a gauntlet of rods in the surf. Note the long flexible rods preferred for pompano.

If you prefer bait fishing, select a medium-heavy to heavy 10- to 11-foot rod with plenty of backbone. Be sure to bring a surf spike with you as it will be tiring to hold it for any length of time, and bait fishing is a waiting game.

Unless you're committed to surfcasting, and know exactly what you want, it may not be wise to put a lot of money into your first outfit. A perfectly serviceable combination can probably be obtained for less than $100. If you get serious about the sport, that can serve as a back-up while you spend more money on top-of-the-line equipment.

Even subtle variations in techniques may dictate the best rod for the situation. For instance, my favorite lure is the pencil popper, and my technique for working it makes a fast-action rod tip preferable to a stiffer one that may be better for metal lures.

Another consideration in tackle selection is where you're fishing. Along open sand beaches there's no need for lots of backbone in a rod for turning a big fish, as you can usually follow along in whichever direction the fish heads. On the other hand, rocky areas may require that the fish be stopped before it runs past an obstruction and cuts you off. Though it's tougher on me physically, I'll select a heavier rod for rock-strewn Montauk Point than I'll use along the central Jersey coast where the only obstruction may be a swimming-limits buoy.

Most anglers discover their preferred combinations by trial-and-error, but that expense may be avoided by seeking advice from fellow surfcasters fishing the same way, in the same places, you intend to fish. I've spent a good many hours on the beaches over the course of decades, but am always looking for ways to do things better. By and large, surfcasters tend to be helpful to anyone seeking advice on the beach. There's no better source of information than that which comes from those actually pounding the surf on a regular basis. Don't be shy about asking for it.

Reel Choices

A wide variety of reels will match up to whatever rod you select, and they don't necessarily have to be very expensive. The internal spool spinners I started with were a problem in the surf, no matter how relatively expensive they were at the time, because surf waves carry sand with them and that quickly works its way into the reel. Washing reels off in fresh water just

Joe Blaze releasing fly-caught bluefish at Ortley Beach, New Jersey.

drove the sand deeper and added to the problem. The development of skirted spools mitigated that situation, and virtually all spinners suitable for saltwater use are now made that way. Sand can still creep in under the spool, but taking a wave isn't the instant problem it used to be.

Most anglers are satisfied with standard spinning reels, but a few don't want to take chances on bail malfunction and opt for manual pick-up models, which require the angler to pick the line with their fingers, rather than relying on a mechanical bail. The top-of-the-line Van Staal spinners come standard in that fashion, but other reels can be converted at tackle shops that specialize in surfcasting. Some top-of-the-line reels, such as the Shimano Stella, feature full bails, but eliminate potential problems with mechanical devices that trip the bail by being built so the bail must be engaged by hand.

LIGHT SURF SPINNING

You don't always need long rods for surfcasting. In many cases, boat anglers may already own rods that will do the job under a wide range of circumstances. That's usually the case along Gulf of Mexico beaches, and surf specialists along the central New Jersey coast also favor shorter, light tackle because light plugs, such as the Bomber Long-A and Yo-Zuri Crystal Minnow, are popular when casting to school striped bass.

The main difference between those rods and standard light 7-footers are the extended handles, which allow easier two-handed casting on those occasions when long casts are required, and allow more leverage, so more pressure can be applied to large fish.

There was always a certain amount of risk involved in using light spinning tackle on the beach when big fish were hooked. It was common to spool up with 8- to 12-pound monofilament lines in order to get a sufficient quantity of line on correspondingly small reels. That's not as much of a consideration now for those willing to use braided lines with their small diameter and high breaking strength, which allows for greater line capacity on smaller reels.

This high break strength also allows the fisherman to apply lots of pressure without breaking off, a characteristic that is especially helpful at the end of the fight when the sudden added stress of landing the fish in the surf can result in a sad conclusion to an otherwise successful battle as the angler grabs the leader to drag his catch up on the sand.

Bluefish taken on Yo-Zuri Surface Cruiser pencil popper, with seeker spinning rod and Shimano Stella reel.

Catching the braided line at bail of Shimano Stella spinning reel using the tip of the index finger. (Joe Blaze photo)

CONVENTIONAL TACKLE

It was all revolving spool reels in the surf when I started. We didn't have any other kind of reels.

As noted in the introduction, backlashes were virtually an every-cast proposition for me as a kid, until I was able to afford better casting reels and developed an educated thumb.

The older generation of surfcasters all used conventional reels, such as the Penn Squidder, in those days until spinning tackle was gradually accepted. Many of the earliest spinning reels just weren't manufactured to stand up to saltwater, and anglers had to wash them immediately after use to prevent them from corroding beyond repair. Conventional reels had smooth drags with lots of capacity for relatively heavy line, could take the abuse, and were no problem for the veterans who had long since paid their dues in learning how to cast them. Heavy conventional rods from 9 to 12 feet were favored, and a few anglers still use that tackle for bait fishing in the surf. The last fisherman I saw routinely casting lures with standard conventional

Design and materials have become more sophisticated over the years, but the strength and reliability of the conventional reel is still an important part of the surfcaster's arsenal.

tackle was the late Hal Lyman (1915–2004; the legendary Cape Cod conventional surfcaster, who along with Frank Woolner, founded *Salt Water Sportsman* magazine) when we fished together for bluefish at Cape Hatteras many years ago.

Baitcasting tackle also involves a revolving spool reel, but they are much lighter, finely tuned, and easier to cast with light lures than conventional reels.

The level wind mechanism on baitcasters lays line on the reel perfectly every time, thus making backlashes less likely. Combined with lighter conventional rod blanks, such as 7-foot popping rods, baitcasting reels are still seen occasionally in the East Coast surf and are commonly used from Gulf shores. Revolving spool reels have much more strength than most spinners, can be cast great distances, and are still a good choice when targeting heavy fish such as sharks, very large red drum, and striped bass.

LINE

The development of tiny-diameter braided lines has created almost as great a fundamental change in surfcasting as monofilament did in the post-WWII

Revolving spool reels are time-proven and still effective at battling large, tough bass such as this one landed by "Crazy Alberto" Knie. (Alberto Knie photo)

days. The debate as to what line is best rages on. Most surf fishermen still use mono, but the advantages of braid are so great that it's well worth putting up with the inconvenience of learning how to use it. PowerPro, Suffix Braid, Berkley Fireline, and other modern braids all provide high breaking strength in a fine diameter with hardly any stretch. That means you can get all the capacity you need on a relatively small reel. Braid doesn't twist like mono, so reeling as the drag is slipping won't result in a mass of tangled loops as soon as the bail is opened.

On the negative side, braid will cut your finger like a knife if you get careless, and only certain knots can be used, as slippage is a big problem with braids. The lack of stretch increases sensitivity, so tiny bumps on a plug that would never be felt with mono can be detected.

Hook setting is also far superior with low-stretch line, though that can also result in more pulled hooks during a fight. Stretch in mono provides a safety factor for the angler in preventing broken lines, but that really isn't a concern in making the switch to braids, as higher pound-tests are normally used. I spooled on 20-pound when I first tried braid in the surf and ended up trying to pick out one wind knot after another before cutting away much of the expensive braid. That didn't surprise the manufacturer's representative who had sent it to me, as he conceded it's very difficult to deal with such fine diameter braid in the surf. He recommended switching to at least 50-pound test, a size that still had smaller diameter than the mono I'd been using. Wind knots are still a problem at times, but they're much easier to get out with heavier tests.

A most important thing to remember before installing braid on a reel the first time is the need to use backing. Failing to first put a few layers of mono or Dacron on the spool will result in the braided line simply spinning around the spool hub. It will not grip the hub, and must be attached to material that will.

Another significant problem with braid involves the likelihood of developing an annoying cut in the fingertip you use to hold the line for the cast. It's hard to avoid that, even with mono, if you're doing a lot of casting. This isn't the cut to the bone that can occur if you put your finger on braid when it's being pulled off against the drag, but it will make for uncomfortable casting. Fishing gloves, a finger guard, or tape on the finger may overcome that problem. You can avoid it by lobbing, rather than snapping, casts. Another solution is to make your mono leader long enough to provide a

Rich Rusznak releasing a bluefish caught with a Van Staal spinning reel. He is using a casting glove for protection from the braided line. (Joe Blaze photo)

few wraps on the reel so you are handling the monofilament when you cast, rather than the braid.

LEADERS

Leaders of heavier strength than the running line should always be used while surfcasting as they help offset fraying from rocks and any other bottom obstructions, provide some protection against toothy critters, and give the angler something substantial to grip when pulling a hooked fish from the surf. Fluorocarbon leader material is expensive, but it blends into water better than monofilament. That's not normally required in the surf, and isn't necessary at all with poppers, but many surfcasters seek any edge they can get. Don't be shy about using heavy pound-tests for leaders, especially when sharp-toothed species such as bluefish are around. Though anglers seeking blues may favor wire leaders even for lures, I've found results are far better by tying the same lures to 80-pound monofilament leaders.

CHAPTER 4

Casting

Like any other athletic activity, casting requires coordination and balance. All too often I see anglers doing a hop, skip, and jump to the surfline before flinging out a wildly inaccurate cast as if they were throwing a javelin, with the rod ending up being held only by the throwing arm. In actuality your body shouldn't move at all except to pivot with the cast.

Strength helps but isn't critical, as proven by many slightly built women who can out-cast most men.

Achieving maximum distance is key to success in surfcasting on occasions, but ninety percent of the time other factors are more important, such as accuracy and using the right bait or lure. There are exceptions in various parts of the world, such as England, where gradually sloping beaches are common and very long casts are needed to reach fishable waters. The specialized pendulum method of casting was developed by anglers there, and popularized by John Holden who wrote a book, *Long Distance Casting*, about it.

Most anglers will do very well with standard casting techniques that can be developed quickly with spinning tackle. Unless fish are feeding wildly just out of reach, or bait must be placed over the outer bar to get a bite, a lob technique should be sufficient to get your lure or bait within payoff range in most areas. For reasons explained in the chapter on reading

Rich Rusznak shows great style as he loads his rod deeply to heave a popper at Long Branch, New Jersey. (Joe Blaze photo)

the surf, there are times when overcasting can be more of a problem than short casts.

The key to getting off a good cast is loading the rod sufficiently and releasing the line at the proper moment overhead so it will sail out over the waves rather than landing at your feet or behind you.

Holding the rod correctly is key to the entire operation. In the case of spinning, place two fingers over the reel seat and two below while using your index finger to control the line by laying it on the fleshy portion of your fingertip for easy release.

To begin your cast, open the bail and let out enough line to drop the lure a few feet below the rod tip. The exact distance is a variable depending on your tackle, but keeping the lure close to the tip will result in a lack of both control and distance. Bait rigs should be assembled so they allow a similar drop from the tip, as you'll find it very difficult to work with a long leader. Get a fix on where you want to cast before swinging the rod behind you and look behind you to insure everything is clear before beginning

Spinning reel bail now opened with line held by index finger. (Joe Blaze photo)

Author initiates cast with rod behind him, preparing to load it for the cast, and checking behind him for safety. (Joe Blaze photo)

Looking toward the target area and preparing to load the rod for the cast. (Joe Blaze photo)

Loading the rod with the weight of the lure and starting the forward stroke of the cast. (Joe Blaze photo)

Rod now fully loaded with energy of forward casting stroke. (Joe Blaze photo)

Author illustrates pulling back with the hand on rod butt to increase the energy of the cast. (Joe Blaze photo)

The author continues to hold the line in the index finger as the lure is overhead and starts its forward motion toward the target area. (Joe Blaze photo)

The author continues to pull back with hand on rod butt, just before releasing line from index finger. (Joe Blaze photo)

In another view the author is pulling the butt of the rod toward his waist to increase the loading of the rod on the forward cast. (Joe Blaze photo)

The author has released the line from the index finger and now squarely faces the target area allowing the line to shoot out from the spinning reel. (Joe Blaze photo)

During the retrieve the rod tip is held high enough to keep the line above the surf waves and the tip is worked with wrist action to activate the lure. The use of the wrist rather than the entire arm conserves the stamina of the angler, especially when many casts are required. (Joe Blaze photo)

During the retrieve the author uses wrist action to impart motion to the lure. (Joe Blaze photo)

At the end of the retrieve the author stops reeling so that the correct length of line extends beyond the rod for the next cast. (Joe Blaze photo)

Author is now prepared for the next cast with the proper amount of line extended from the rod tip. (Joe Blaze photo)

the cast. Move the rod forward in a steady motion to get it completely loaded before releasing the line overhead. A properly loaded rod will have a deep bend that stores the energy just prior to releasing it as the rod springs forward.

Conventional casting is similar, though an educated thumb is required in order to prevent the kind of backlashes that plagued me as a youngster. Today's revolving spool casting reels are more finely tuned, and very little thumb pressure is required during the cast. Indeed, during a smooth cast, the thumb shouldn't touch the spool at all until the sinker or lure hits the water. This is when the spool rotation must be slowed or stopped to prevent a backlash that will occur on even the finest reel.

Follow-through is essential to a good cast. For instance, if you're right-handed, the left arm should be pulling down on the butt of the rod as the right is powering forward. There's little extra effort involved in this method, but it will make a big difference in distance achieved.

The author uses tackle matched to the conditions at hand on the Sea Girt, New Jersey, beach. (Joe Blaze photo)

FLY-CASTING

Fly Tackle

The entire range of fly tackle may be used in the surf, though it's mostly the heavier gear, made expressly for saltwater that best meets the special demands of this fishing. It's not just a matter of dealing with larger and stronger fish. Most standard fly tackle designed for fresh water won't withstand the corrosive nature of saltwater.

Joe Blaze of Brielle, New Jersey, is a veteran fly-fisherman who has fished around much of the world, but puts in most of his time on central New Jersey beaches and jetties simply because they're within minutes of his home. He recommends a 10-weight, 9-foot fly-rod, though others prefer a 10-footer. The reel shouldn't be very expensive, so you won't get too worried when you inevitably drop it in the sand and scratch it up. An intermediate fly line covers most situations, and works best in the surf,

Fly-fishing at the tip of Sandy Hook. (Joe Blaze photo)

partially because it has a thinner diameter than floating line. It also stays under the surface so it isn't moved around by waves. The reel should be large enough to hold the fly line plus 150 to 200 yards of 20- or 30-pound Dacron backing.

Tie in a 12-inch section of 25- to 40-pound monofilament ending in a Perfection Loop to the end of the fly line so pre-prepared leaders can be easily attached.

Standard fly-casting techniques are used in the surf, but the conditions make it much more challenging. A very important point for fly-rodders to remember is that they're probably not alone on the beach. While your concentration is on the watery target out in front, the backcast is going just as far behind you. It's essential that you look behind on every cast as not everyone is aware that a hook may come whizzing by as they innocently walk down the beach well behind a line of anglers casting with spinning or conventional tackle.

I'm not a fly-fishermen, but Joe Blaze is accomplished in that art from both boat and surf. His description of this unique and rapidly growing sport follows:

Fly-Casting as Lure Delivery

Fly-casting *is* lure fishing. Flies are a type of lure and fly-casting is another way to deliver a lure to the fish. The advantages of fly-casting can also be its weaknesses, so picking the situation when fly-casting is the best choice is part of the fly-fisher's skill set.

Some fly-fishers exclusively fly-fish, so they may sacrifice fishing effectiveness to make their fly-fishing "point." Some do this as ego-burdened purists, while others exclusively fly-fish because fly-casting is fun in itself. One can always fly cast, but it may not always result in fish caught. At the right time and place, fly-casting can be the most effective way to catch fish.

Advantages and Disadvantages of Fly-Casting:

- Fly-casting can accurately deliver very small flies to the fish.

- Fly-casting can accurately deliver very light flies to the fish.

- Fly-casting can deliver very flexible, undulating flies to the fish.

- Fly-casting can deliver flies to the fish with subtle, prey-imitating action.

- Fly-casting can deliver sound-producing flies to the fish, such as rattle flies and poppers.

- Fly-casting can deliver flies to the fish at controlled depths through the use of fly lines, which float or sink at specified rates of speed.

- Flies are relatively inexpensive compared to other lures, especially if they are tied by the angler.

- Fly-casting can only rarely deliver flies to the fish at over 100 feet from the angler.

- Fly-casting can only rarely deliver flies to the fish at over 50 feet of depth below the surface.

- Fly-casting only rarely uses overall line strength greater than 20-pound, although sections of the line can be reinforced for durability.

- There is no biggest possible fly, but flies that exceed eight inches long or are particularly bulky, like poppers, can be difficult to cast at maximum distance or for long periods.

- Heavily weighted flies are measured in grains or grams, not ounces or kilograms.

- Unless scented or sound-producing flies are used, effective fly-casting requires conditions where fish can see the fly.

- Fly-fishing has disadvantages in heavy surf which some find hard to overcome.

- Windy conditions are either a help or hindrance depending on the skill of the fly-fisher and the wind direction and intensity.

The Fly Line

The fly line is selected according to the fishing conditions, species sought, and type of fly to be delivered. For mild surf conditions, e.g., tropical flats fly-fishing, floating or slightly sinking lines of lighter weight are often selected with a double or forward taper which is just sufficient to deliver the desired flies, but not so heavy as to disturb the target species. For heavy-surf fly-fishing, a heavier fly line is often selected with an aggressive forward taper to handle the wind and waves and deliver larger flies to the fish. Some fly-fishers feel that an intermediate or sinking fly line is best in the surf for several reasons: because its diameter is less than a floating line, it cuts through the wind better; it sinks just below the breaking waves so it stays put and maintains better tension to reveal strikes; and since it is beneath the surface, it avoids floating vegetation.

The Fly-Rod

Fly-fishing in the surf requires many casts and longer casts than other types of fly-fishing. To accomplish this without fatigue the angler uses the entire body including the legs, back, shoulder, and arm muscles. Using only the arm muscles for saltwater fly-casting may lead to subsequent joint problems or excessively large biceps.

The ideal in saltwater fly-casting is to aerialize the maximum sustainable amount of fly line with as few back and forward fly-rod strokes, known as false casts, as possible.

This ability to cast a long line quickly is valuable when the position of the fish is rapidly changing or when surf conditions limit the casting opportunities. Being able to deliver the fly with as few fly-rod strokes as possible can also be a big advantage when many casts are being made, reducing fatigue and extending the fishing period.

Fly Reels for Surf Fishing

The fly reel is used to hold the fly line and is used when fighting the fish to retrieve the line. It may have an adjustable drag, but drag for fly-fishing is seldom more than a few pounds of resistance. For surf fly-fishing choose a fly reel made of non-corrosive materials which has its mechanism protected from entry by saltwater or sand and is easily washed and maintained. The most expensive and complex fly reels are not ideal for surf fly-fishing because of the inevitable wear and damage due to sand and saltwater intrusion. Maintenance of the fly reel after every use by washing and appropriate lubrication will significantly extend the life of the reel.

A length of fly line backing up to several hundred yards, depending on the overall reel capacity, is attached to the reel spool arbor. This backing is usually thin braided Dacron or Spectra of 30- to 50-pound test. To the backing is attached the rear end of the fly line using a loop-to-loop connection or an Albright knot. To the front end of the fly line is attached the leader butt using a loop-to-loop connection or an Albright knot. The leader, made of fluorocarbon or nylon and from 3 feet to 12 feet long, can be tapered or not. The leader ends in the class tippet section that's the weakest part of the fly line system. The test of the class tippet is generally 2-pound to 20-pound test, with 12-pound or 16-pound test the most commonly used in surf fly-fishing.

SPECIAL CONSIDERATIONS FOR SURF FLY-CASTING:

Safety

- Always wear some form of eye protection when fly-casting.

- Always use spike-soled footwear when fly-fishing from slippery rocks, jetties, bulkheads, or groins.

- Fish with a companion when the location has deep water, slippery conditions, fast currents, heavy boat traffic, or other hazards.

- Look behind you on every cast so no bystander is injured. Others are often not aware that the backcast portion of the fly cast can extend considerably behind the fly angler and that the velocity of the fly can approach 100 mph.

- When fly-fishing in a crowd, de-barb your hooks by flattening the barb with pliers.

- Protect your skin from the sun and wind, especially when the fishing trip extends over several hours.

Fighting Fish in the Surf

Landing a fish in the surf using as fly-rod is actually easy when you take advantage of the wave action to beach the fish. In this method the rod is used to direct the fish's head first toward the beach. The fly-rod is not used to actually pull the fish out of the water and up the beach. The waves and water carry the (tired) fish up onto the slope of the beach. When the water recedes, the fly-fisher can grab the fish and drag it farther up the beach.

To avoid breaking your fly-rod when fighting or landing a fish, the angle formed between the tip of the rod and the butt must never be less than 90 degrees. Depending on the rod construction and materials, as this angle approaches 180 degrees (i.e., the tip is pointing back at the rod butt), the rod will invariably break.

Fighting the fish with a fly-rod is different than with other tackle. Keeping the rod tip high may work with other tackle, but that advice, though picturesque, is not appropriate. The only powerful portion of the

A fly-fisherman takes a high vantage point when taking on the surf at the north jetty of Manasquan Inlet, New Jersey. Elevated position allows plenty of room for backcast and presentation of the fly.

fly-rod is in the butt section of the rod and it provides virtually all of the fish-fighting resistance of fly tackle. When holding the fly-rod to fight the fish you will feel the most substantial resistance when the rod handle is held relatively high, the rod is tilted up off the horizontal slightly and the tip is pointed directly at the taut line to the hooked fish. The pressure on the rod is mostly on the (heavier) butt section and not the (thin and unsubstantial) tip section of the fly-rod. This is what is meant by fighting the fish with the butt of the rod. Any attempt to raise the rod tip higher will not increase pressure on the fish, but will merely put more bend in the rod closer to the tip. So fight the fish with the butt section of the rod. The battle will be over quicker and a healthier fish will be released to fight again, unless of course regulations permit the taking of a particularly tasty fish for your supper.

In the surf the fly-fisher should fully retrieve the fly into the wash. Many times fish will follow the fly long distances and strike at the last possible moment. There are numerous methods used to retrieve the fly line and fly to attract the fish. Observe other fly-fishers to get an idea of the variety of retrieves possible. If one method of retrieve is not working, switch to another style. Keep experimenting with the retrieve until the fish hits your fly.

The striking pressure of fly tackle, using either the rod to strike (not recommended, as it can pull the fly away from the fish if it misses the initial strike, or strikes short) or strip striking with the line handling hand (recommended), is quite minimal. Therefore use flies with high quality, light wire hooks that have been properly sharpened. Heavy hooks with blunt points or excessively high barbs are very hard to set into a fish using fly tackle.

Hooks over size 3/0 require heavier fly tackle to set into the fish properly.

CHAPTER 5

Lures for the Surf

Just about any lure used from a boat has probably been tossed into the surf at one time or another, except for bunker spoons and high-speed offshore lures. Deep-diving plugs are also impractical, due to the difficulty of casting the long, diving bill and the shallow environment in which a deep running plug can be a nuisance.

The same applies to very heavy versions of metal lures such as diamond jigs, though smaller sizes work surprisingly well considering diamond jigs are designed to be worked up and down off bottom rather than cast and retrieved.

PLUGS

Many of the plugs favored by striped bass surfcasters were designed by such early-casting legends as Stan Gibbs and Bob Pond during the post-WWII era. Though duplicated and refined by many lure makers since then, they remain just as effective on the modern breed of stripers.

While plastic plugs are pretty reliable out of the box, every wooden plug seems to work a bit differently. Anglers should check them over carefully in the water before depending on them. The metal swimming plate generally shouldn't be altered. If they don't swim properly, use pliers to

Alberto Knie used a surface lure to capture this striper. (Alberto Knie photo)

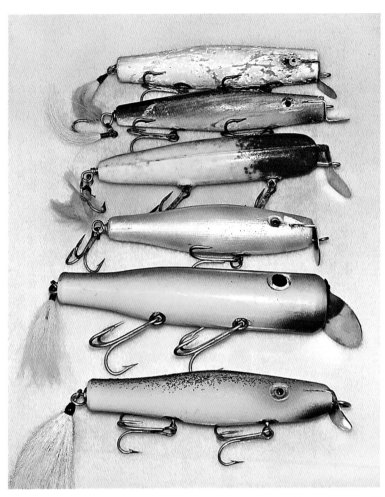

Topwater plugs, in a variety of shapes and colors. The second from the top will swim deeper due to the angle of the lip. Action can be adjusted by bending the attachment eye to alter the swimming action on the retrieve. (Joe Blaze photo)

slightly move the eye, where you fasten the line, until the swimming motion is correct. Most anglers use a snap to facilitate changing lures. That also allows a plug free movement, but many fish have been lost due to snaps that came open during the fight. I prefer to tie poppers directly to the leader, to eliminate that possibility. Snap swivels tend to interfere with plug action and aren't necessary to prevent twist. Snaps must be of high quality and heavy enough to stay closed even when pressure is greatly increased at the moment of landing a fish.

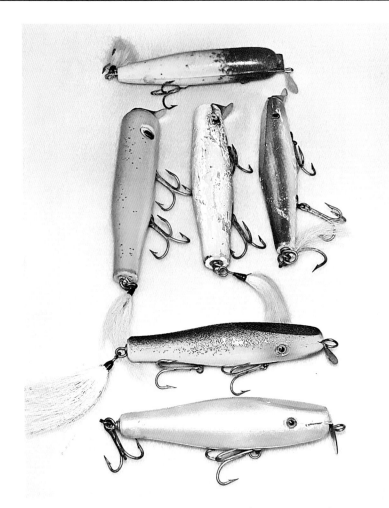

A selection of large surface and sub-surface plugs. (Joe Blaze photo)

Use at least 20-pound fluorocarbon leaders for small swimming plugs and 40- to 60-pound-test for larger swimmers. Monofilament is good enough for poppers, as the leader is out of the water, and not easy for the fish to see. With subsurface lures, fluorocarbon is much harder for fish to detect, and can be a lot more effective.

Don't forget a small quality barrel swivel at the other end of your leader, which should be short enough to provide the proper drop off the rod tip for casting without fouling in the top guide.

When choosing plugs, be sure they have wired-through construction rather than screw eyes that are likely to get pulled out of the lure, especially by fish that tend to twist during the fight. With through-wire construction, fish can be landed even on a broken plug.

Though the barbs on hooks are there for the purpose of securing fish, they also represent a threat to the angler. That's especially the case with the typical three treble hooks on plugs. The late Al Urban was a legendary boat-casting specialist who drifted just beyond the range of surfcasters off the south shore of Montauk, Long Island. He used the large Atom 40 swimmer on conventional gear to raise big stripers from rocks 20 feet and more below the surface, but every one of those plugs had the barbs crushed so they could be backed out in case he ever got one in his hand. Urban felt that if he maintained proper pressure during the fight, he didn't lose any bass, while at the same time ensuring his own safety. Crushing the barbs is even more important with toothy fish such as bluefish that thrash around and often snag anglers concentrating more on avoiding their teeth, as I can testify from sad experience!

Cutting down on the number of hooks may be possible, but be aware that the manufacturer balanced the plug for the hooks it comes with. Removing one could affect the action, though snipping off two points of a treble shouldn't be a problem. In any case, check the swimming action after making any changes.

Understanding how the species you're seeking attacks a lure is helpful when making alterations to your lures. Most predators strike at the head, so it's the first treble that's most important. Striped bass fishermen often eliminate the tail treble or replace it with a large single hook dressed with bucktail.

On the other hand, if you're seeking the toothy bluefish, which tend to chop at the rear to disable their prey, it's the rear hook that's most important, and the forward trebles may be removed.

Another way to avoid getting a hook in your hand isn't recommended. I was driving along the Jersey Shore one fall day when I saw a blitz of big bluefish develop at Seaside Park. Grabbing a Yo-Zuri Surface Cruiser out of its box, I quickly tied it onto my surf outfit and rushed to the surf for an instant hook-up. The expected action was forthcoming on every cast as I jumped one jumbo blue after another. Some were on long enough to make a run, but all were lost while anglers around me were

The author tying on a Yo-Zuri Surface Cruiser popper and testing the knot. (Joe Blaze photo)

A variety of plastic plugs suitable for light tackle surfcasting. (Joe Blaze photo)

beaching their fish. Finally, I took a good look at my plug and noticed the plastic hook guards Yo-Zuri had put over each treble point. Since it's difficult to back them off, I ended up tearing them off the points as best I could with my pliers, and my fish catching quickly improved.

Pencil Poppers

I had the privilege of not only learning to fish plugs from the late Stan Gibbs, but also of seeing how much goes into making a wooden plug. Gibbs himself didn't realize there were so many steps involved until I had him write them all down one day. I believe it came to over forty separate steps per plug, which is why quality wood plugs are so expensive.

Gibbs had the ideal testing ground for his creations almost in the backyard of his home and woodworking shop near Cape Cod Canal.

Gibbs designed the pencil popper in a shape that maximized casting distance and imitated a fish fleeing in such a panic that it's mostly out of the water. After learning how to work it, the pencil popper has become my favorite lure.

The trick is to use a spinning rod with some tip action (often characterized as "fast action") and a long butt. Let the butt rest against your thigh while working the pencil popper by using constant wrist motion with your right hand around the reel seat as you take up the slack with your left hand on the handle. Since there is no pulling motion as with standard poppers, I find it possible to work pencil poppers all day without tiring.

While there's nothing more exciting in surfcasting than watching a fish slam any popping plug, the pencil popper is my favorite since it's basically out of the water and strikes tend to be even more furious. I've been the Pied Piper of the Pencil Popper, often being the first to use it in areas from Mexico to Australia. Especially when Japanese and French anglers took a liking to it, that lure quickly became an international favorite. The Yo-Zuri Surface Cruiser became a big seller throughout the world.

There is no popping head in the pencil popper, and it's designed to create commotion with its bulbous rear end. That constant wrist action churns the water as the plug skitters along the surface. A fast retrieve is generally best, but one night on Gin Beach at Montauk, Long Island, I grabbed a pencil popper in the dark instead of a darter when bluefish were

Poppers come in a variety of shapes, but are all fished the same way on the surface, to imitate wounded bait fish. (Joe Blaze photo)

hitting. Working it with a darting motion, the pencil popper produced a big blue every cast before I noticed my mistake.

Pencil poppers can be slowed considerably for a trailing fish that won't commit by reeling only a few turns to maintain some movement while increasing the tip action and virtually making it dance almost in place.

Lower your rod tip when doing this so it will be possible to strike when the fish hits. Many game fish have taken pencil poppers after following for some time, but stopping it completely for even an instant rarely works.

Any game fish that eats large live baits can be attracted to pencil poppers. I've used them to catch species ranging from striped bass and bluefish in the Northeast to roosterfish, cubera snapper, and the various jacks and trevally in the tropical Pacific.

During early summer 2006 there was a great run of jumbo striped bass under schools of bunker along the northern New Jersey Shore, and big pencil poppers were deadly when 20- to 50-pound bass were actually pushing those bunkers to the beach. While boaters were able to get into those fish regularly, surfcasters had to be ready whenever the bass decided it was time to push bunkers (also known as menhaden or pogies) into shallower water where they could corner them and successfully inhale those 2- to 3-pound bait fish. Big pencil poppers don't look anything like a bunker, but when the feeding frenzy started all that mattered was getting the big popper out into the middle of the massacre, and pencil poppers can be cast the proverbial mile. Watching stripers that size explode on a pencil popper is a thrill not to be forgotten, just as is the case with a jack crevalle in Florida, cubera snapper in Costa Rica, or roosterfish in Baja California.

Pencil poppers come in a great variety of colors, and some are really beautiful. I'm often asked what color is best for a particular species, and my answer is "Whatever appeals to you, because I can't imagine it makes any difference to the fish." Not only are fish color blind, but if they could see the color or even the shade on a pencil popper you're not working it correctly! All they should see is the thrashing butt end and a swinging treble hook. Birds may prefer a certain color, but my only preference is for something bright that makes it easier to follow the plug in low light conditions or rough water.

The Gibbs Pencil Popper is still being made in wood by his successors, and several craftsmen also turn out very good versions in wood. Cotton Cordell was fishing with me in the Bahamas several decades ago when he asked me what my favorite lure was. After talking about the pencil popper (which Gibbs never patented), he went back to Arkansas and made his version in plastic, a hollow plug containing beads for a rattle effect. Stan Lushinsky, who books the Ixtapa / Zihuatanejo fleet in Mexico, swears by the Cordell pencil popper for roosterfish.

Traditional Popping Plugs

Standard popping plugs feature a large cupped head that creates a popping noise when yanked. In most cases, a fairly fast retrieve with lots of jerking works best, but a slower retrieve is often advisable at dawn and dusk. The Atom Striper Swiper is a typical standard popper that Bob Pond first made in wood, but soon developed as a bestseller in plastic. Stan Gibbs created the Polaris, a popper with even better casting characteristics, and there have been many other variations of the basic popper.

Another similar surface lure is the chugger, with an even larger cupped head to create more commotion. Chuggers are generally worked slower and with harder yanks to throw lots of water and raise game fish from the depths. They involve more work, and some don't cast well, but they tend to attract large fish. The Yo-Zuri Surface Bull is a heavy chugger-type that can also be worked as a pencil popper. As a general rule, standard poppers and chuggers work better in rough water than pencil poppers that tend to tumble.

Yet another popper variation is the Ranger, a flat-sided plug that doesn't pop while creating a commotion as it's dragged across the surface. Its casting characteristics are excellent, making the Ranger a good choice when having to cast into the wind. The single-hook rigging is also perfect for fish with teeth. It doesn't look like much, but the Ranger is the only surface lure I've ever hooked a cruising Pacific sailfish on. Unfortunately, the Cabo spinning reel I cast with at Hannibal Bank didn't have enough capacity and that Ranger was last seen headed toward Panama's Isla Coiba.

Among the many plugs Stan Gibbs devised, two others deserve special mention. His original swimmer was shaped with a lip so it could be cast as well as a popper, but provided a swimming action. That became a very popular plug with the pros who cast from the rocks under the Montauk Point Lighthouse, and ever since been referred to as the "bottle" plug. Those anglers also swore by another Gibbs swimmer with no lip: his Darter-type. Gibbs had to refer to it that way because Creek Chub's famed Darter had been on the market for many years. The latter has long been a favorite of snook and tarpon fishermen in the South, and is still as effective these days.

That wasn't the only southern plug to inspire northern surfcasters. The Boone Needlefish caught on in the New Jersey surf when the long, slim sand eel became the primary forage fish during the 1970s. Though the

Another bluefish that fell for the author's Yo-Zuri summer cruiser pencil popper at Long Branch, New Jersey. (Joe Blaze photo)

shape was right, I've never understood why striped bass were fooled by a stick-straight lure when they were seeking the undulating sand eel. Nevertheless, they did work when reeled slowly along or just under the surface with very little action other than an occasional movement of the rod tip. The original needlefish were all small, slim lures, but surfcasters in Rhode Island, Block Island, and Cape Cod started turning out much larger variations with heavy-duty hooks that fooled quite a few trophy stripers.

Though they don't cast well, large metal-lipped swimming plugs can be worked slowly to provide a deadly surface action that often attracts lazy game fish with an undulating movement. It's a thrill to see big boils come up behind those lures even when the fish doesn't actually strike.

Bob Pond created the big Atom forty-some years ago for conventional casters, and downsized a bit to the Junior Atom for spin fishermen. Those plastic lures are still standards, and there are many wooden metal-lip swimmers created by local craftsman that provide similar actions.

Pond also created a unique big plug for conventional casters when squid were the prey of choice. The Reverse Atom was the swimming plug reversed so the fat portion (without the swimming plate) was at the end. Furthermore it was constructed with chambers that had holes to take in water. That created a heavier lure for those who could cast it, and the lure also squirted water as it was worked back-and-forth on the surface.

While big plugs attract big fish when they're focused on large baits, the vast majority of predators are attracted to the surf by the presence of small, schooling bait fish. Imitations of that small bait will produce game fish ranging from striped bass, bluefish and weakfish to snook, spotted sea trout, red drum, and corbina most consistently.

Every area has its own favorites, but MirrOLures, especially the 65M, the Bomber Long A, and Yo-Zuri Crystal Minnow are among the most common light-tackle plugs employed.

As previously noted, I don't think color makes any difference in pencil poppers. It's only the usually white bottom of the lure that fish can see from below, not the decorator colors on top. With swimming plugs there often seems to be a difference in results under various circumstances with different colors. The general rule is to use light colors during the day, and dark (particularly black) at night. As noted in chapter 9, I had more faith in my white Junior Atom on a Halloween night at Charlestown Breachway, Rhode Island, and enjoyed a night to remember with stripers of 38 and

32 pounds that hit under the full moon. Perhaps all the light from the moon made it seem like day, but I've also done well trolling white swimmers on wire line at night on Montauk's Shagwong Reef. Once I start catching fish on a particular plug, I tend to fish it until the lure fails me.

My personal feeling with all lures is that action, size, and profile are all more important than color. Just as with a fly-fisherman working a stream for trout, surfcasters should try to duplicate the "hatch." If the predators are on slim, 3-inch bait fish, chances are they will ignore a 10-inch popper that might drive them crazy under other circumstances.

Soft Plastics

Some of the most effective lures developed in recent years have been soft plastic swimmers that provide the best of swimmers and jigs in one bait. The shads manufactured by companies such as Tsunami and Storm have become the dominant fall lure for striped bass that are feeding on young-of-the-year menhaden, often referred to as peanut bunkers.

This class of lure consists of special jig heads with a soft, flexible body molded over them to form a lure with great action at almost any speed. They cast well, and can be fished very slowly off the bottom or speeded up to stay just under the surface. From a boat, shads can even be jigged or slowly reeled off bottom. Though quite a few stripers can usually be caught on a single lure before it is damaged beyond use, it may only take one blue-fish to destroy the body and render the specialized jig head useless.

The DOA Baitbuster has long been my favorite for casting from the sides of Florida bridges for tarpon, and it also works in the surf. Whenever possible, I prefer using lures like the Baitbuster and shads that have only a single hook, as these do little damage to fish that are going to be released, and as well are much safer to remove from an active fish.

Lead-Head Jigs

Often simply referred to as bucktails, lead-head jigs come in many forms and with various dressings. Basically designed to be bounced off bottom, they can also be steadily retrieved with a jerking motion. Bucktail is the most popular dressing, but various synthetics will also work, and many anglers prefer to add a piece of Uncle Josh pork rind for additional action.

Plastic baits provide lifelike bait fish action. With toothy species like bluefish, though, their useful life can be short. (Joe Blaze photo)

The development of Berkley Gulp lures has provided an ideal tipping for jigs as they provide both action and scent.

Plastics ranging from shad bodies to worms may also be added to lead–heads that provide the casting weight and a means of presenting the lure. Almost any predator will hit a lead-head of some sort as the attractor can be changed to provide varying lengths, colors and profiles; and the lure can then be retrieved fast along the surface or slow and deep.

There are quite a few variations in jig heads from the flattish Upperman jig to bullet-nosed designs and all will work in the surf. SPRO has developed its Swimming Jig that's a shaped body covered with a 3D

Bob Noonan with school bass caught on Finesse soft lure on lead head at Sandy Hook, New Jersey. This bass carried an American Littoral Society (ALS) tag—covered with moss at the vent. (Joe Blaze photo)

design and rigged with a single Gamakatsu hook. The variations on jig design, colors and materials are nearly endless.

Metal Lures

Metal is easy to cast and deadly on a wide variety of species, as such lures can be worked fast or slow in order to cover the desired depth. If there were just one lure I had to select when fishing the surf, it would have to be a metal. Such lures are versatile and attractive to virtually all predators. The strike is rarely as spectacular as on a surface plug, but hook-ups are more certain and fish usually don't twist off as easily.

The hammered stainless steel Hopkins Spoon is the standard of metal lures since it's virtually indestructible, won't rust, and will last indefinitely if not broken off or stolen by some toothy critter. It comes in both the slim Standard and Shorty versions, either plain or with various dressings, and rigged with single or treble hooks. I prefer single hooks as they appear to be just as effective while not seriously harming fish to be released, and they

Antique block tin squid lures. "Metals" have been an important part of the surfcaster's arsenal since the sport began.

pose less of a threat to the angler. Bucktail on the hook makes the Hopkins more attractive, while a tube is a better bet for bluefish, as they tend to hit at the back end rather then the head of the lure, thus keeping the teeth away from the mono leader and preserving an expensive lure.

The Acme Kastmaster and Luhr Jensen Krocodile are a couple of the other metal standards, and these have more built-in action than the Hopkins. As previously noted, the angler can vary the retrieve to accommodate the situation. A fast retrieve along the surface will elicit strikes when game fish are actively chasing bait on the surface, but more fish are generally caught when the metal is allowed to sink a bit before the retrieve is started. A slower retrieve with more tip action may be called for if the fast retrieve is ignored or short strikes result. When fish aren't showing, it may be worthwhile to slow the retrieve considerably so the lure works just over bottom or even kicks up some sand. Obviously, great care must be exercised in doing so on a rocky bottom where the possibility of hanging up is a consideration. That slow, deep retrieve may also attract species other than the surfacing game fish usually sought. Aggressive bottom species such as the summer flounder will frequently hit metal lures.

Old-timers used much different metals. The lead squid was a slim lure with a single large embedded hook in the tail. The lure could be bent to get the action just right. The block tin squid followed that, and usually featured a swinging hook on a split ring. Though tin tarnished easily, those lures could be polished by rubbing them in the sand or scraping them with a dull knife.

Teasers

Placing a fly or another type of lightweight lure ahead of the main lure has become almost standard procedure for surfcasters over the last few decades, especially since Tony Stetsko landed the largest surf striper ever: a 73-pounder on Cape Cod that hit an 8-inch black Deceiver rigged ahead of the lure.

In addition to flies, slim plastic lure bodies such as the Felmlee eel can be rigged on a hook as a teaser. Any teaser will interfere with the cast, so if distance is important it may be best to eliminate it. On the other hand, many fish are caught close to the wash where the weightless teaser is most effective as wave action gives it motion at the very time the heavier lure is losing its action.

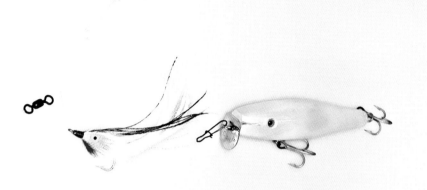

Creek Chub plug with a fly teaser in front of it, rigged in tandem on monofilament leader, sets up the illusion of a chase, enticing predators to strike. (Joe Blaze photo)

Flies

Just about anything a fly-fisherman would cast into a stream or lake, except dry flies, will work at some time in the surf, though anglers are advised not to depend on flies with very light wire hooks under such rugged conditions.

Joe Blaze emphasizes you still need relatively light-wire hooks with small barbs to set them with the limited pressure of a fly-rod. He feels length, silhouette, and weight, which determines sink rate, are more important factors than color. Blaze advises lengths ranging from 2 to 10 inches with a variety of materials ranging from really soft and flowing like marabou to stiffer feathers or plastic hair. His favorite silhouettes cover the range from a thin worm / sand eel to the intermediate profile of the Lefty's Deceiver, to a bulky squid / herring / bunker style that's weighted with lead eyes as designed by Bob Clouser, or Bob Popovic's Jiggy Bead Head.

A few light, streamlined poppers with plenty of hook gap between the point and the popper body are also good to have. Blaze notes he always carries too many flies and uses only a few—but at least they don't weigh much!

Summer flounder (fluke), like this caught by Joe Blaze at North Beach, Sandy Hook, are well suited to fly-fishing.

A small Lefty's Deceiver fly makes a close match for the peanut bunker (baby menhaden) that draw predator species into the surf. (Joe Blaze photo)

CHAPTER 6

Bait Fishing

Bottom fishing in the surf requires a lot more effort than it does from a boat or pier where lines are simply dropped to bottom. In the surf, not only must the bait and rigging be cast, often for considerable distances, but it must be kept in place in the payoff zone while waves do everything possible to wash it back to the beach.

Surfcasters fishing sand beaches would have an even harder time overcoming that problem if the pyramid sinker hadn't been developed. The flat top and pointed end of the pyramid digs into the sand and resists being pulled out by waves. There are also regional variations of the pyramid with the same anchoring purpose in mind.

The shape that makes the pyramid ideal for digging into sand also creates a problem in rough bottom. Do not use them in rocks. There are also times when a bank sinker is preferred in the surf. Rather than anchoring bait in place with a pyramid, it may be more effective to cast the bait with a bank sinker and then follow it along the surf. Standing in one spot will result in the rig being carried into the surf rather rapidly, but it should remain in the payoff zone if you follow the drift. Keep in mind the fact that many fish feed right at the drop-off. That's particularly true of fish feeding on clams. Though clams are highly desired by everything from small bottom fish to trophy striped bass, those fish rarely see a naked clam in nature.

Fishing natural bait in the surf has its own challenges and skills to acquire, but pays off in consistent catches. (Joe Blaze photo)

Natural bait rigged below a pyramid sinker and a well-executed cast provide the simple formula for success. Joe Brooks casts natural bait rigged with a pyramid sinker. (Jack Woolner photo, courtesy IGFA)

Storms push clams up on the beach, where they die. The surf recaptures those clams not consumed by sea gulls at high tide, and provides the opportunity for game fish to feast on them right in the undertow. This is why kids often catch large stripers even though they can't cast far, while adults cast far out and overshoot the fish.

It's often possible to pick up clams for bait off the beach after an easterly storm, but check local regulations before doing so. In some places you may need a clamming license, or shellfish gathering may be prohibited. That's the case in New Jersey where areas around old sewage outfall pipes that have been inactive for many years are out-of-bounds, while clams washed up a few yards away can be picked up by those with a clamming license.

I've never had a problem casting fresh clams, as they're fairly tough. Use large hooks and run them through the meat a couple of times before adding the stringy lips so they will wave in the current. Be sure plenty of hook is exposed. If the clams are large, I prefer cutting them in half, even if both pieces are to be used on the hook, as that exposes more scent.

Casting a sinker alone would be no problem, but adding bait and rigging creates a lot of wind resistance. Thus, every effort must be made to streamline the rig, unless distance is of little concern. Long leaders are definitely out and usually aren't necessary anyway in the roiled conditions common to the surf.

New Jersey anglers using clams often utilize a fishfinder rig. That consists of a plastic slide, with an attached snap for the sinker, through which the line is passed to a swiveled leader that permits a fish to pick up the bait and run with it as the line passes through the slide. Others prefer a double hook set-up with two dropper loops tied in above the sinker and a hook inserted in each loop. The sinker is placed in a loop at the end, and the entire rig is relatively easy to cast. That's also similar to the rig used by pompano fishermen in Florida who must make very long casts to the outer bar. In most cases, fish will hook themselves even with the rod set in a sand spike: a plastic or aluminum tube with a pointed end to dig into the sand.

Bluefish (in upper right of photo) about to blast into a school of rainfish.

Sandworms rigged for striped bass bait with pyramid sinker on fishfinder clip.

That's especially the case when circle hooks are used. It's a bit harder to bait up with non-offset circle hooks, but they're very effective and allow for unharmed release of small or unwanted fish.

Anglers often fish more than one rod with bait, setting them in sand spikes so they can cover more of the beach. When placing the rod in a sand spike, be sure the drag is backed off enough that a hooked fish won't be able to pull the rod down and drag it into the surf. I learned that lesson the hard way one day as the rod I had just placed in a sand spike, while casting the other, bent over and was dragged out to sea just a few feet out of my reach. I was only catching school striped bass, and suspect the fish responsible probably wasn't very large. Sand isn't concrete, and it doesn't take much to bend a sand spike over until the angle becomes critical and the rod is pulled out. The rest of the way is downhill, and it happens fast!

Almost any fish or shellfish and be used as bait in the surf. Every area has its favorites, and that's a likely basis for making your selection. Smaller fish generally favor small baits such as seaworms, shrimp, and strips of squid or clam. Larger fish favor more substantial fare such as baits cut in chunks or strips from fish, the heads of those fish, and whole shucked clams. Fish heads are effective and relatively easy to cast with the hook placed through the lips. It's been my experience that heads are most effective only with the guts still in them. Crabs and small fish will eat those guts without the angler

Allen Riley using clams for striped bass on Raritan Bayshore. (Allen Riley photo)

feeling anything. Thus, the bait must be checked frequently. If crabs are a problem with smaller baits, slim cork floats may be run up the leader to hold the bait above bottom and at least make it a bit more difficult for them to get at it. Sea grass is a problem in some areas, particularly after a storm. If you see grass washed up on the beach, you can be pretty sure that it's also covering your bait. The best bet then may be to move. It's not uncommon for one stretch of beach to be almost unfishable with weed, while another only hundreds of yards or a few miles away may be free of weed.

Bay anchovies (rainfish, or Anchoa mitchilli*) occur in the estuaries and near-shore ocean of the mid-Atlantic coast of the United States. Individually this bait fish is easily captured by predators, but in dense schools sufficient numbers survive predation to remain a significant forage for East Coast game fish like striped bass, bluefish, and weakfish.*

Small live baits, such as the bait fish known as spot, which is a favorite along the along the Mid-Atlantic coast, are prime fare for a variety of predators, but are hard to deal with for surfcasters without a beach buggy that is equipped with live-bait holding tanks and re-circulating pumps.

Large live baits for the most part, are difficult to present in the surf. An exception is the eel, as their slim shape is ideal for casting and can endure lots of abuse while continuing to remain lively. In addition, eels are very easy to maintain and handle for surfcasting. Keep them cool and moist, and they'll live for hours out of water. You can transport them in a plastic bag filled with moist seaweed and placed on ice in a small cooler that's convenient for carrying to the surf or out on a jetty. Be sure eels are separated from the ice, as they'll drown in water depleted of oxygen. Carry a dry cloth for handling the slimy eels. Keeping them on ice will also slow them down for hooking, though they'll recover rapidly in the water.

The usual method of hooking eels is from the lower jaw up through an eye socket, though some surfcasters feel they work better while anchored in the surf when hooked through the tail section. Head-hooking is the way to go when fishing eels from jetties, so they can be cast and retrieved like a lure. The same applies from canal shorelines. Wet suit anglers at Montauk swim to outlying rocks, and carry spare eels in a plastic bag along with a tackle bag containing lures and extra hooks and leaders so they never have to leave their hard-earned perch in order to re-bait.

Another means of acquiring the proper live bait in the surf is to snag individuals from passing schools of bait fish. Schools of menhaden (known locally as bunkers, as pogies in New England, and fatbacks in North Carolina) travel close to the beach at times, especially when pushed in by large predators. Large leaded treble hooks are cast over the schools, allowed to sink a few feet, and then retrieved in a sharp sweeping motion to snag the tightly schooled forage fish. When a bunker is snagged, the bait is free-spooled on the spot because the weight of the generally 1- to 2-pound fish is too great to cast out again. If a big striper or blue is present, it will often grab the injured fish even though hundreds more uninjured bunkers are available. There isn't any need for a long drop-back, especially if the predators are sharp-toothed (as in the case of bluefish) or if you plan to release the catch. This has become a common means of catching large striped bass and bluefish in the New Jersey surf. If the specialized weighted snag hooks aren't available, a snagging rig can be constructed with a plain

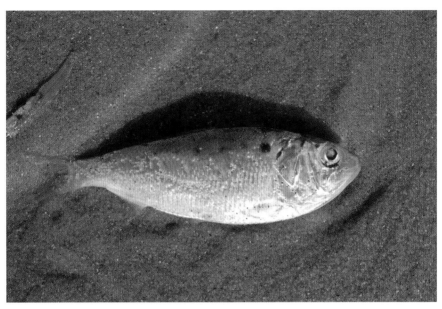

Peanut (juvenile) menhaden (Brevoortia tyrannus) *—also known as pogy or mossbunker— is a plankton-consuming prey of Atlantic coast game fish which occurs in large schools of uniform sized individuals in estuaries and coastal waters. All sizes of menhaden are targeted by game fish, from juveniles of 2 to 6 inches up to full-sized adults at 12 to 16 inches.*

large treble by adding a drail (a long sinker, often available with swivels at both ends) or egg sinker for casting above a swivel to a short, heavy leader to the treble.

A similar, scaled down, rig is used for snagging much smaller forage fish such as young-of-the-year bunkers, usually referred to as peanuts. Those fish would be missed with a large weighted treble or torn up by it. The casting weight should be as light as necessary for casting, and also serves to keep the bait in place long enough for predators to find it before moving on.

Those smaller baits can also be re-cast, though they'll have to be re-hooked through the lips to facilitate both casting and presentation. Even more efficient is a cast net when small bunkers are close to the beach, as is common from late summer into the fall. Most schooling bait fish aren't as easy to snag or cast net as bunkers, but it's worth the effort if large predators are in the area.

Bunker-snagging rig. Additional egg sinker weight increases sink rate and casting distance, though the weighted treble is usually sufficient by itself.

Throwing cast net from the north jetty of Sebastian Inlet, Florida. This is an efficient method of getting a good supply of bait fish, but requires some practice to perfect the art.

Any large bunkers you end up with can be turned into a first-class dead bait as they still have the natural slime on them. Cast the head out on a fishfinder rig, or use chunks from the midsection. Though frozen bunkers are often effective, there is no substitute for very fresh bait. Veteran striper pro D. J. Muller of Manasquan, New Jersey, learned that lesson while fishing bunker heads and chunks at night from a local beach when his friends were catching trophy stripers. All he was catching at the same time were dogfish (small sharks), until he realized that the successful anglers were using fresh-caught bunkers. At the time there were lots of bunker schools just offshore, and boaters were snagging bunkers during the day to catch large stripers below them. Since a fresh bunker could be snagged on every cast, they had plenty to spare. Muller had the boaters save him bunkers with the slime still on them, and was soon beaching big bass, including a 50-pounder.

In some cases, the bait you need may well be right at your feet. Pompano fishing is very popular along the east coast of Florida as those small fish are a gourmet's delight. The best bait for them is almost always sand fleas. Those tiny crabs scurry back-and-forth along the surfline, and can be caught by hand. It's much more efficient to use a special heavy rake with a wire basket attached. Hundreds of sand fleas can be raked up quickly from prime stretches of beach right where you'll be fishing.

Specialists in northern New Jersey use similar rakes to harvest calico crabs. Whereas sand fleas are fine bait in their natural state, stripers desire the much larger calicos when they're in the tender shedder or soft-shell state. Those specialists don't rake many that are just right, but set up tanks in their garages to hold the crabs until they're at the right stage for bait.

Calicos are fine in their hard-shelled state as cut bait for crab-eating fish such as tautog. Blueclaw crabs are also fine for those fish, and can be purchased at fish stores as well as caught from bayside docks. Fiddler crabs are excellent small baits for the same species, and they can be chased down as they scurry between burrows in marsh banks that may be close to shore-casting areas.

Mullet are prime bait fish in the fall all along the Atlantic coast from Long Island to Florida. They may be caught with cast nets from the surf, especially in pockets next to jetties. Mullet make fine live baits for predators such as striped bass, and are effective dead baits for bluefish.

Mole crabs, also known as sand fleas, on pompano rig ready for the Florida surf.

The crab rake has captured plenty of mole crabs for pompano bait in Florida. Anglers work the rake along the edge of the surf for fresh live bait, a pompano favorite.

Mullet bait and wire-leader rig with pyramid sinker for surfcasting for bluefish.

BAIT FISHING FROM JETTIES

The presentation of live baits is much easier from jetties. Indeed, it may be possible to bring those baits to the scene. Northern New Jersey jetty specialists are often able to buy live herring or bunkers from local marinas and transport them one at a time out on the jetty in a bucket full of water. Obviously, they won't live very long under those circumstances, but all the effort is worthwhile if a big fish is in the balance. Other anglers build carrying tanks in their vehicles in order to transport live herring they catch during spring herring runs and preserve in tanks or plastic swimming pools, with pumps to circulate the water, in their garages.

Jetty fishermen also use live eels. They're a natural bait at night and can be cast time and again and still stay lively. Eels remain usable when fresh-dead and still flexible. The angler can impart a little bit of action with the rod tip during a slow retrieve. After all is said and done and the eels have long since expired, the eel skin can be rigged on a special head to create a very effective lure that once was a standard, but is now rarely used.

Since the jetty you're standing on is a fish attractor, it's not important to cast great distances. Unless there are scattered underwater rocks at the end of the jetty, the predators you seek are as likely to be right at your feet. Always cast that eel alongside the jetty before working away from it. Bottom fish, such as tautog in the northeast, feed on crabs and other shellfish along the jetty, so your bait should be close to the rocks. Use egg or bank sinkers, rather than pyramids, in order to avoid constant break-offs. Heavy sinkers usually aren't necessary, and some veteran jetty anglers use old spark plugs. They're either tied on with lighter line, or the leader to them includes an overhand knot that will break easily when they become snagged on the rocks, so the bait is not lost along with the sinker.

Great care must be exercised in fishing jetties as the tidal rocks in many areas are covered with a slime that may be difficult to see, but will cause nasty accidents. Broken legs and teeth are among the lesser difficulties arising from carelessness when fishing from jetties. Always wear cleated waders, or strap-ons such as Korkers, when traversing anything except high, dry rocks. Even then it's important to walk carefully as stepping between rocks can cause as much damage as slipping.

Jetties at the mouths of inlets present a unique opportunity to fish both live baits and large dead baits that couldn't be cast from shore by using the outgoing tide to transport them out to sea. Shark fishermen use balloons and big floats to drift large fillets or chunks of bloody fish to their quarry, and can utilize big game tackle with plenty of capacity since they don't have to worry about casting it.

CHAPTER 7

Surf Accessories

The classic view of surfcasters in waders with a plug bag and various accessories hanging off a belt may be the reality at times, but a great deal of surfcasting is much more casual. That's especially the case during warm weather, when my outfit consists of fishing shorts, a shirt with a pocket for my reading glasses (a necessity for old-timers when rigging), and bare feet.

It's a real pleasure to be able to fish the surf under those circumstances as I get lots of exercise and can enjoy the freedom of movement while covering lots of ground. Most surfcasters carry a lure bag (canvas covering a series of plastic or aluminum lure holders) over their shoulder, but I don't like that weight, and usually only utilize a few lures in any case. The few extras I carry are enclosed in used Ziploc baggies that are slipped into the shirt pocket or my pants along with a tape for measuring fish and the minimal terminal tackle necessary to take care of a possible break-off, such as a few yards of leader material plus some swivels and snaps.

The only problem is how to protect my cell phone. That's become an important fishing item for the surfcaster, as the blitz you're looking for may be only a phone call away. It can be wrapped in a baggy and placed in the back pocket.

Having freedom of movement is wonderful, but modern lightweight chest waders are almost as good when cooler weather arrives. Neoprene

When fishing action is hot and the blitz is on, preparation and waders get forgotten as anglers rush into the surf to catch the action while it lasts. (Joe Blaze photo)

waders are pretty comfortable, but you're not going to be doing much running around in them without sweating and getting tired pretty quickly. There's a world of difference with lightweight waders. While they won't keep you as warm in cold weather, that problem is taken care of by the clothing underneath. I've switched to Snowbee XS lightweight waders,

A surf bag is standard equipment for surfcasters. It is carried over the shoulder, keeping lures and other tackle out of the way, yet within easy reach. (Joe Blaze photo)

and could never go back to heavy models. They come in various sole selections, but I opted for the cleats that provide the option of being able to go out on slippery jetties. With other soles, you'll have to strap on Korkers in order to do that safely.

Though I started surfcasting decades ago in hip boots, those aren't seen along the surf very much anymore. Yet, especially on weekends, I still see lots of anglers running back and forth to the edge of the surf in knee boots or even just sneakers. That may not be the ideal thing, but it's comfortable, and even somewhat practical on calm days. Small fish can be cranked up on the sand, and who cares about getting wet while landing a big one!

The other important accessory to have with you is a pair of fishing pliers. I carry ProFishCo pliers, in the belt case they come with. Pliers are not only handy when re-rigging, but also while removing hooks. That applies not only to sharp-toothed fish, but with any fish when treble hooks are involved. Take it from one who has made a couple of trips to the emergency

Al Ristori, right, and John Bushell, Jr. (owner of Betty and Nick's Tackle Shop in Seaside Park, New Jersey). Al is wearing lightweight, breathable Snowbee waders, while John is wearing traditional, plastic-coated, heavyweight waders.

room, it's all too easy to get hooked by a flopping fish with that second treble! Plugs are especially dangerous when a teaser is used ahead of them, and the fish is on the teaser. Hook outs are even better for removing hooks because you can keep your hand farther away from the fish or poke it far down the throat to remove a swallowed hook.

I always try to carry a Hook out when expecting to deal with sharp-toothed fish. It can be tucked inside the belt, or carried in the pocket within your waders. That's also where my bag of spare lures and terminal tackle and the cell phone go. A good waterproof scale can be added for release fishing if the tape measurement isn't good enough. An alternate means of measuring fish is with your rod. Simply lay it alongside the fish and check to which guide, wrapping, word (from the brand name or rod specs) it reaches. Then take the measurement when you return to your vehicle. If keeping fish is a consideration, you can mark your rod with the minimum size for a quick decision.

Ristori using cell phone to keep in touch with the surf action—an essential piece of gear when waiting for word of a blitz. (Joe Blaze photo)

Using a hook remover puts less stress on fish whenever the removal requires a delicate touch, even if they are not hooked deeply.

Author with a big striped bass at Long Branch, New Jersey. When everything goes well, and the right equipment is at hand, this is the surfcaster's reward. (Joe Blaze photo)

Another handy item that can fit in your pocket is a nail clipper. They can be purchased very cheaply at discount stores, and replaced when they get too rusty, but are the handiest tool with which to cut lines and trim knots. A pocketknife is also advisable for the rare circumstances where you'll have to cut something, but remember to wash it off in fresh water when you get home.

If bait fishing is in your plans, then a standard 5-gallon bucket is ideal for carrying everything you need. Stick your bait, rigs, sinkers, sand spikes, and a knife into the bucket to carry out to the beach. Most beaches have enough debris on them to provide a board for cutting purposes, but if that's not the case, you can add one to the bucket. Cutting V-shaped notches around the edge of the bucket will provide hangers for lures and rigs. Once at your spot, the lid can be replaced to provide a seat, or if you only have a few items, they can be removed and the bucket upended for seating. Finally, the bucket can be used to carry your catch back home.

Only short sand spikes are suitable for carrying in a bucket. If you prefer longer sand spikes, drill a hole toward the top of each and string a long loop through them so they can be carried over your shoulder or attached to the rods you're carrying.

Sand spikes can be tied together for easy transport along the beach.

Extra-long sand spikes are useful to raise the line above the water when the waves are running high.

Gaffs aren't usually required for surfcasting, as anglers can generally use the force of waves to slide their catch up on the beach. Those anglers who feel they need one can purchase short-handled gaffs that are little more than a large hook with a handle on the shank, plus a short strap for attachment to a belt. A spring wire protector may cover the point, or the angler can use a cork or piece of tubing for that purpose.

Author shows how to use a stainless steel Shorty Hook Out tool to remove the lure from a bluefish. The extended reach of the Hook Out avoids the dangers of the razor-sharp teeth of the fish. (Joe Blaze photo)

A longer gaff is important when fishing jetties, as it's often dangerous to scramble down to the water in order to land a big fish. Jetty regulars carry longer gaffs strapped to their backs so they're not impeded when walking. Such gaffs can be bought, or constructed from a broken rod with a large barbless hook wrapped on the end.

Jetty fisherman at Manasquan with jetty tools: Long gaff on bamboo pole, rag, lure bag, Korkers and short boots for walking on slippery rocks, rain suit, stringer for his catch. (Joe Blaze photo)

Night fishermen require some form of illumination, especially during the dark of the moon. Lights with straps to be used on the head are handiest, and others are made with clips that can be secured to the bills of fishing caps. I like the lightweight, waterproof Ameripack light that has a clip for carrying in a shirt or pants pocket, and operates with a push of the button at the end. It can easily be held in the teeth when both hands are busy.

Just as a light is essential at night, sunglasses are a must when you get on the beach in the morning. Once the sun comes up along the East Coast you'll soon find it to be very uncomfortable to stare into it for very long. It's very tiring, and your ability to read the beach or spot fish swirls and other signs of life will be impaired. Be sure your sunglasses are polarized as that will cut the glare and enable you to look into the water to spot schools of bait. Rig them with holders of some sort so they won't be lost, and can be dropped down to your chest for better vision when rigging or taking off fish. Sunglasses also serve a safety purpose as they protect the eyes against hooks or lures that pull out in the wash and may project toward your face.

Insects can be a problem on some beaches, especially during calm early mornings and evenings. There may also be localized problems you'll soon find out about, such as a southwest wind that blows bloodsucking green flies out of the marshes and onto the beaches along the Jersey Shore in the summer. Therefore, it's wise to carry some insect repellent for such circumstances.

If you're into keeping large fish and aren't operating from a beach buggy, several yards of light rope will facilitate hauling your catch off the beach. Drag them in the wash, so the water helps reduce the drag, until it's time to make a straight shot to your vehicle, by which time you'll probably regret ever keeping them.

There are occasions when it's possible to catch fresh bait in the surf. Cast nets are standard equipment for some surfcasters. These are generally small mesh nets for small bait such as the young-of-the-year mullet or menhaden (locally known as peanut bunkers) that migrate south along Atlantic coast beaches in the fall. If you don't have a beach buggy with an arrangement for live bait, a few small fish can be kept alive in a bucket full of water that's changed frequently. In any case, you'll have the freshest bait possible, which is always preferable to frozen. In some situations it's possible to catch much larger live baits, such as "corn cob" mullet and adult menhaden, with large mesh cast nets.

Sometimes using a net means untangling hooks and possibly missing the best action of a blitz. (Joe Blaze photo)

Specialized rakes can be used to catch crabs on the spot for bait. Though they're heavy to carry to the surf when a beach buggy can't be used, there's generally no need to move far from the spot you're fishing. This is an important tool of the trade while fishing for pompano with sand fleas.

CHAPTER 8

Beach Buggies

The history of beach buggies has never been recorded, but Hal Lyman and Frank Woolner, founders of *Salt Water Sportsman* magazine, noted in their *Striped Bass Fishing* (Winchester Press, Piscataway, New Jersey, 1983) that, "Over-sand vehicles have been evolving ever since a few adventurous pioneers stuck balloon tires on Model A Fords well before World War II." It was after the war when the idea of cruising the sands to seek fish gained popularity, and the readily available Model A quickly became the popular choice. Other light two-wheel-drive vehicles were also used, and walk-in trucks soon drew interest. Then there were war surplus four-wheel-drive vehicles, though Lyman and Woolner noted they were hard to maintain because their parts differed from civilian models.

Four-wheel drives have taken over almost completely since then, as driving in soft sand is difficult enough even with that great advantage. Whereas those original beach buggies were second cars, most anglers today can afford only one. Therefore, they generally buy new four-wheel drive vehicles, such as Jeeps, or station wagons, vans, and light trucks that have all the creature comforts for the family as well as the off-road capability. Maintenance is a much bigger problem with the new vehicles. Rustproofing is essential, along with a wash-down (especially for the undercarriage) after each use in the salty environment.

Beach buggies and their owners take up residence at Barnegat Inlet, New Jersey, for the weekend. (Joe Blaze photo)

The art of beach driving is soon acquired by those who pursue the sport, or they quickly take up some other form of recreation after expensive tow jobs or drowning their vehicle.

While good tread is necessary for driving on roads, that just makes it easier to dig in on the beach. Since most beach buggies have to be driven home, and may even be family vehicles, a compromise has to be made. A tire gauge is the most essential tool of the trade. Air pressure in the tire is reduced to 16 to 18 pounds (depending on the weight of the vehicle) before going on the beach, and then replaced before returning home. The more air eliminated the better, but there must be enough to keep the tire on the rim. The weight of the vehicle is spread over a greater area, and the driver is literally able to float over the sand rather than digging in.

Slow acceleration and no braking are keys to staying on top of the sand rather than bogging down in it. All traveled beaches have tracks laid down by other buggies. Stay in those tracks and you shouldn't have any problem, but be alert that you don't follow them too close to the water on a flooding tide or end up in a rut. Driving very slowly will avoid lots of potential problems on the beach.

Accelerating when you get stuck will only make a bad situation much worse. Start taking preventative action right away if you find yourself

Some of the many beach buggies with permits for Island Beach State Park, New Jersey. The ideal track lies between the surfline and the loose, deep sand more inland. Existing tracks will show you the way. (Joe Blaze photo)

Using a beach buggy gives the angler access to more remote areas of the beach. (Joe Blaze photo)

The comfort a well-equipped buggy means late-night bluefish can get the angler's full attention. (Charlie Fornabio photo)

bogged down, such as digging out around tires and placing boards under them so you can get back on track.

The number of beaches where beach buggies are allowed has greatly diminished, and in many cases they're only available on an off-season basis with a permit. The owner will probably be required to have certain items in the trunk that enable him to provide his own assistance when stuck. This should include a shovel; a hydraulic jack with a square board to place under it; other small boards to be placed under tires; a tow rope; a fire extinguisher; and a powerful flashlight.

A basic consideration in beach driving is the tide. The harder sand is close to the surf, which makes for easier travel, plus that's where you'll be fishing. However, always be aware of a rising tide and higher waves created by an offshore wind. Don't get so distracted that water gets up to your tires. Park high and dry, but do get out of the track so other drivers can utilize it.

The well-equipped beach buggy has plenty of rod holders to keep the right equipment at the ready for any action that might develop. (Joe Blaze photo)

A properly rigged beach buggy allows the angler to cover areas not available to those on foot, to enjoy some heat during cold weather plus food and drink at any time, and can also be a giant tackle box on the beach. A rod rack on the front bumper keeps completely rigged rods ready for instant casting. A rod rack on the roof is a second choice as it's not quite as convenient as just dropping a completely rigged rod into the rod holder at the front of the vehicle.

Though rods are generally safe when placed on a roof rack, there was one time when that didn't work out for me. I was driving back from fishing North Bar at Montauk Point with Bruce Newmark when a deer jumped over the car hood and shattered the windshield with its rear hoof. Newmark managed to drive almost back to the house we were staying in, with his head out the driver's side window, when he realized the rods weren't on the roof. Fortunately, there wasn't anyone else on the road in the middle of the night. When we got back to the scene of the incident, the two rods were still lying in the middle of the road, and Newmark managed to salvage one reel and one rod from the casualties.

By parking the buggy facing toward the surf, a rod rack can also be used in place of sand spikes. A cooler rack is often added on the bumper to hold your catch. These can be constructed of PVC or aluminum, and commercial units are available at tackle shops. Plastic lure boxes can be stacked in the rear of the buggy to accommodate lures and terminal tackle. If live-bait fishing is a consideration, a tank can be set up in the rear, or the bumper cooler can be converted.

Some larger buggies include sleeping accommodations, and campers can be added to the truck bed of four-wheel-drive pick-up trucks. Beach regulations must be checked as only active fishing is permitted at night in some areas.

Along much of the New Jersey coast it's possible to gain many of the benefits of beach buggies without ever getting your vehicle near the surf as most of the northern Shore is built up along the beach. Street endings can be checked out and the car parked if working birds, swirling fish, or bent rods are spotted. Even when I had a four-wheel-drive SUV, I opted for that clean alternative as it's a lot easier to cover ground on the road, and there's a huge improvement in gas mileage.

Beach buggies can be a good clue as to where the fish are. A concentration of them can be spotted from quite a distance, and keeping an eye on

John Green rigging a surf spinning rod in the holder of his beach buggy at Island Beach State Park, New Jersey.

A tire pressure gauge is an essential piece of equipment when driving on the beach. The dressed out beach vehicle has everything the angler needs accessible, and preferably on the front bumper.

John Green selecting terminal tackle from the extensive selection in his beach buggy. The rear of the ideal buggy functions as a giant rod rack and tackle box, on wheels.

them should soon indicate whether their owners are actively fishing or just talking about it. Also watch for movements of buggies along the beach. A steady movement in the same direction may be an indication that something is happening along that way.

CHAPTER 9

Reading the Surf

When I was younger, the surf appeared to be all the same and my only concern was casting as far as I could over the waves. Of course, that's not at all the case. Being able to read the surf is what separates the pros from amateurs on the beaches.

If you walk to the surf on a calm day at high tide you might well feel that it's all the same. Yet, returning six hours later will provide a different perspective, as bars and sloughs uncover at low tide.

Thus, when learning any area you should first check it out at low tide. Predators are likely to be seeking prey in the cuts between bars that also provide them with the security of depth. As the tide rises they may move right up on the bars as they flood, if that's where the bait is. Your best bet when nothing is showing is to work those cuts or "sloughs" that may no longer be as obvious as the ocean fills in. A bit of wind and large waves will help identify the hot spots where your efforts should be directed.

Beautiful, placid surf is rarely good for fishing, especially with lures. You want waves breaking on the bars and washing into the cuts. Predators that frequent the surf learn to feed when current and waves create churning conditions that confuse their prey and make it easier to assault them. As a result, your efforts are most likely to pay off when the current is running rather than at high or low tide.

Configuration of rocks and sand along the shore provide clues to the bottom topography, and the location of both bait schools and predator species. (Joe Blaze photo)

The latter is usually the least likely time to find predators within reach of the beach, though in many areas it's possible to wade far out to fish the outer bar as the tide drops. Rather than casting into cuts, you're now casting to open ocean. That may be productive as predators at times are reluctant to come into the surf, or there may not be enough bait there to draw them in. But it's also dangerous.

The path to the outer bar may be barely passable for just a short period while the tide is at its lowest. Inevitably, it will begin flooding with the incoming tide, and the change of depth in an area of breaking waves may be imperceptible as the water level rises behind you and is over the tops of your waders on the return trip.

Current isn't usually visible along the beach, but is very important in terms of feeding activity. At the mouths of inlets and rivers it is much more than very important: it's everything!

Current determines how and where you can work lures. Reading the tide tables will give you a pretty good idea about when currents will be running. From low tide to high it will rush into the inlet before slacking and then turning out. However, there are many exceptions to the rule.

While learning striped bass fishing during the early 1960s, I traveled through New England selling Garcia fishing tackle to wholesalers and

Bluefish hitting a popper right on the drop-off just yards from the angler, demonstrating the importance of working the lure all the way back to the wash. (Joe Blaze photo)

Tom Fote wading the surf at Island Beach State Park, New Jersey, with a typical early-season bluefish which feed heavily on their way north up the coast. Note stripping basket to hold loose fly line and keep it out of the surf. (Joe Blaze photo)

Joe Brooks makes a long cast with conventional tackle to clear the breakers in this classic photo. (Frank Woolner photo, courtesy IGFA)

making courtesy calls on fishing tackle dealers. That gave me the opportunity to fish such fabled areas as Charlestown Breachway in Rhode Island. When the waters boiled out of Charlestown's saltwater pond through the narrow jetties, anglers would line up at the tip and cast plugs or jigs across the mouth so they were drawn seaward to stripers sucking up bait fish dropping out of the pond before being slowly retrieved against the current. A rotation was established so everyone's lines were being retrieved in turn and massive tangles could be avoided.

An unusual aspect of the tide at Charlestown Breachway is that it drops for about three hours before the current swings into the desired outgoing mode. Though I never caught a large bass during the few times I fished shoulder-to-shoulder at the tip of the jetty, I once had a great Halloween night there doing everything wrong.

Returning from Cape Cod after a northeast storm to my home, which was at that time on Long Island, I stopped overnight to fish

Surf anglers working a school of bunker between two jetties at a Deal, New Jersey, beach. (Joe Blaze photo)

Blitz between two jetties, with birds circling over the same bait schools that the fish attack from below. (Joe Blaze photo)

A surfcaster wades to shore from the outer bar with a bluefish. The anglers in the lineup fishing the outer bar must be aware of the stage of the rising tide in order to cross the trough that lies between them and the beach before the water rises over their waders.

Charlestown in a cold, clearing northwester. While eating dinner I read the tide tables and noted the high tide was conveniently soon after. Returning to the motel, I put on layer after layer of warm clothing (this was before good lightweight insulated undergarments were readily available) and proceeded to the Breachway where I was surprised to find the parking lot almost empty. It wasn't until I waddled out on the jetty that I saw the current roaring in and remembered about that three-hour difference!

Since I couldn't cast under those circumstances at the tip, and had spent too much time getting dressed, I decided to at least make a couple of casts to the backs of the waves rushing toward the beach on the east side of the jetty. The full moon cast a glow on those waves being pushed up by the strong northwester, and my white Junior Atom swimmer was sticking out like the proverbial sore thumb on the backs of the waves when a big bass rose up and engulfed it. There was no more stunned individual on earth at that moment than I.

Surfcasters at Bay Head waiting for bunker schools being worked by boats to come within their reach from the beach.

Long casts are not necessary when feeding predators follow the bait in close on the beach. (Joe Blaze photo)

Anglers on the dunes overlooking the beach compare notes while waiting for the next blitz. Shared information is an important part of surf-fishing strategy. (Joe Blaze photo)

Fighting the striper to the rocks wasn't difficult, but I was wondering how I was going to scramble down into the rocks and land the fish with no gaff when a head popped up down there. There was an angler staying out of the cold wind while swimming an eel, and I hadn't been aware of his presence until the very point I needed another miracle. He gaffed that bass, and another one a half-hour later before I walked off with the two largest stripers I'd ever caught from shore up to that point.

After driving back to Freeport, Long Island, the next morning, the fish were weighed by Ron Fuering at Sea Isle Tackle at 38 and 32 pounds. Ironically, despite ideal conditions, nothing of size was caught at the end of the jetty on the proper outgoing current that night. Sometimes it's better to be lucky than good!

CHAPTER 10

The Thrill of the Blitz

Surfcasters almost always have to work hard for every fish they catch, particularly the great game species. Yet, there are times when we know there will be a hit on every cast as predators tear into schools of panicked forage fish that often jump onto the sand in their effort to flee certain death. Dedicated surfcasters call that a blitz, and we live for those rare occasions when we're on the spot as it happens.

Striped bass are the kings of the northeast surf, and a difficult target for even surf pros, except during the rare, and usually brief, periods when they gang up on bunkers, herring, bay anchovies, and any other schooling forage fish. Then it's a mad scene as anglers race along the beach to keep up with the massacre occurring before it comes to an end.

At times it's mostly schoolies chasing small bait. But size of the fish you find in a blitz can vary greatly. Sometimes large bass school up to attack schools of forage fish, even when the bait fish themselves are not necessarily any larger than usual.

That was the case a few years ago in November when I joined Tom Fote in his beach buggy to seek migrating stripers at New Jersey's Island Beach State Park. I had enjoyed some action on foot, casting to school stripers that morning before meeting Fote at Betty & Nick's in Seaside Park for a quick lunch. After driving into the park, we quickly spotted a

This is the blitz up close and personal. Bluefish school launches the attack on a school of rainfish (bay anchovy) just off the beach. (Joe Blaze photo)

blitz already in progress. There was no question about what was going on, as there were dozens of buggies in a small area, and every angler was actively fishing. Fote moved in front of the other buggies in order to stay ahead of the blitz, and I jumped out as soon as he stopped to run for my rod in the bumper rack. Birds were diving on swirling fish along the outer bar, but they were well within reach as I cast a Tsunami shad into the commotion. I would have been shocked if I didn't get a hit from those fish feeding on young-of-the-year menhaden that we call "peanuts." These were the right kind of stripers, 15 pounds and up; and they didn't disappoint.

There was an almost-instant hook-up on every cast, but no time to really enjoy the fight as I worked hard to beach and release each striper in order to get back out in hopes that the next one would be even larger. My best was a 30-pounder, and I didn't notice any larger than that one. Just about every rod would be bent one minute, then only a few, as the fish steadily moved south and anglers ran back to their buggies to get ahead of the action once again. Then, as suddenly as it started, there were only a couple of bass being fought, and the blitz was over.

Bluefish blitzes are more common along the Mid-Atlantic and southern New England coasts. I've seen the same thing happen with Atlantic jack crevalle in Florida and Trinidad, and with Pacific jack crevalle in Panama and Costa Rica.

On another fall day with Fote at Island Beach State Park, it was solid big bluefish up to almost dark as we cast poppers for maximum sport with 10- to 15-pound blues blasting the surface lures on every cast, even when there was no sign of feeding activity.

Quite often I've walked into bluefish blitzes that remained contained within a relatively small area, so I was able to continue casting blind instead of being forced to run down the beach with the diving birds in order to keep up with fast-moving choppers. Normally ravenous under such circumstances, blues generally hit anything thrown at them during blitzes. Single-hook metal lures work best, as they're easiest to cast into a wind or high surf, and safest to remove. However, it's hard to beat the thrill of a bluefish blasting a popping plug. Even the missed strikes are memorable. Just be sure you have pliers or a Hook Out along in order to free the treble hooks.

Even during such wild feeding activity, there are rare occasions when it's necessary to exercise some ingenuity. In one instance I was having a

Birds wheel over the rapidly moving bait school with birds while this angler is left behind, fighting his fish. (Joe Blaze photo)

hard time drawing strikes during a bluefish blitz on peanut bunkers that were so thick I snagged them on my single hook as I retrieved the lure. It wasn't until I hooked a couple of them through the mouth on that lure, and lobbed it out so they wouldn't tear off, that I was able to hook some of the largest bluefish I've ever hooked in the surf.

All this was nothing new, as Van Campen Heilner detailed in 1946 in his book *Salt Water Fishing*. Though primarily a big game fishermen, Heilner also appreciated the thrills of bluefishing in the surf.

All rods hooked up during a bluefish blitz. (Joe Blaze photo)

Rich Rusznak uses the waves to beach a striper during a blitz at Island Beach State Park. (Joe Blaze photo)

"Fishing for blues from the beach is my favorite way of taking them. Take one of those crisp days in the autumn when the sedge grass is starting to turn and the snipe are trading down the beaches and the mosquitoes and greenhead flies are but a terrible memory. Speed to the coast and climb the dunes and down the other side to the creamy surf. That's bluefish time and bluefish weather.

Pretty soon you'll see a flock of gulls working close inshore. You run as fast as you can and when you reach the spot you find the water being churned into fury by the slashing rushes of a big school of blues. Cast right into the middle of the *school and reel like hell. Zow, you've got one! And your rod bends way down from the shock. Out of the water he comes, shaking his head like a tarpon. In the undertow he dashes back and forth like a fury and on the first wave you drag him kicking onto the beach. He unhooks himself, but you stop only long enough to boot him out of the reach of the waves and you cast again. Over and over the same. Sometimes the school works well off and you have to put everything you've got into your casts to reach them. Sometimes they're rushing about in the undertow at your very feet. Bluefish have the blood madness. They continue to kill long after their appetites have been satisfied. They continue to kill as long as there is anything there for them to kill. They will stuff themselves to the gills, then disgorge and start all over again. As long as you can see the fish you will get strikes. It's thrilling, it's hard work, and it's damn good fun."*

Heilner used the Ford Model T as a beach buggy, and kept two of them in service, one at Cape Hatteras, and the other near what is now Island Beach State Park. His advice was "Cruise slowly up and down the beach, watching for the telltale gulls that denote the presence of a school of blues and then go to it."

In defense of this technique, he offers a memory that all surfcasters hope one day to share.

"One day in September a bunch of us, eight cars to be exact, were cruising slowly along the surf near North Point o' Barnegat looking for blues. Each 'beach buggy' was equipped according to the owner's particular fancy; some with no tops, others with seats like a jaunting car, painted the colors of the rainbow, but mostly aluminum or metalicote, bait boxes on the rear, rods in sockets on the sides, all with oversize tires and all stripped for action.

"Suddenly, as if in unison, the cry burst above the roaring surf, 'There they are! Blues!' Eight exhausts burst into a staccato roar and eight ancient vehicles rushed headlong over the dunes toward the dipping gulls a mile away. We happened to be at the lead at the start and reached the fish first and without stopping to shut off the engine, leaped into the surf fully armed with rods already swinging. In clouds of sand the other buggies quickly arrived and their occupants rushed to the water's edge. For a few minutes the air was full of singing lines and flashing squids and the big blues commenced to dot the sands in all directions. Then as suddenly as they had risen, the school sank, and gathering up our fish we commenced our slow promenade once more.

The bite is on and Rich Rusznak bends into a bluefish on the beach at Long Branch, New Jersey. (Joe Blaze photo)

"Near sunset the other cars left us and we were alone. Way down the beach my partner spied a bunch of gulls whirling and dipping in close to the beach. We headed for them full speed, but when we reached there, no fish were breaking, though the birds were still circling about and making an occasional swoop to the surface. Our first two casts produced nothing and then on my third I had a savage strike and almost immediately into the air sprang a magnificent blue. Twisting and shaking his head like a terrier he contested every foot of the way to shore. In the undertow he seemed to hold fast for a moment and even took some line. Then I got him coming on the front of a wave and landed him high and dry above the surge. A beautiful 10-pounder. My cup was full. If I didn't catch another blue all fall it really didn't make any difference."

Angler in shorts working a popper through school of bluefish attacking bait in the surf at Ortley Beach, New Jersey. (Joe Blaze photo)

Though the thrill of the blitz remains the same today, there are some things that have changed dramatically since Heilner's time.

First of all, the dunes are sacrosanct today. Vehicles may only enter and exit the beach at designated spots. Even walking on the protective dunes is generally prohibited. Then there's the matter of high-speed runs to the fish. Even in the excitement of a blitz, speed limits must be observed on the beaches. On the positive side, that 10-pound blue Heilner was so proud of is now often just an average-sized chopper.

When I was a youngster, adult bluefish were rare. Even trolling a 3-pounder was a thrill. They started coming back when I returned from the Navy, and just kept getting larger until 10- to 12-pounders became routine at times. Many line-class world records were set during the 1970s and 1980s, with the North Carolina surf in late fall and early winter a particular hot spot for blues over 20 pounds. Though such super-sized blues became rare, it still takes a 15-pounder or better to draw any particular notice, even from the surf.

Though bluefish blitzes are more common, it's not unusual to encounter blitz fishing with both blues and stripers mixed together. That's especially the case during the fall migration. One fall I followed the steady movement of peanut bunkers just over the drop-off heading south in the Normandy Beach area, as school stripers practically brushed my waders, shadowing the bunkers in the same direction while bluefish hung just outside the school of hapless bait fish. A long cast with a small swimming plug would produce an instant hook-up with a blue, but casting along the beach attracted the stripers.

It was sometimes difficult to distract the predators as they blasted into the abundant forage. Anglers casting snag rigs enjoyed good success at the head of the school by snagging and dropping, but lures were often ignored with so many live targets available. I had more success under those circumstances by casting a swimmer or popper behind the school, where the stripers and blues were picking up the scraps.

Fall has traditionally been prime time for striper blitzes in the Mid-Atlantic and New England, especially when herring arrive late in the season as the large size of those forage fish tends to attract trophy stripers.

The presence of schools of adult bunker from late spring into the summer along the New Jersey shore has created a relatively new, but explosive fishery for surfcasters. At times it's necessary to cast a snag hook out

Jerry Fabiano caught this school striper with its tail bitten by a bluefish at Island Beach State Park, New Jersey. Often during a blitz several species of predators will attack the same school of bait. (Joe Blaze photo)

into the bunker school and let that large bait swim around until a big bass nails him. However, the greatest thrills occur when a school of big stripers pushes bunkers toward the beach. A big popper or surface swimmer cast into the commotion at that time will usually result in an explosion and instant hook-up. That opportunity occurs most often early and late in the day, but can happen any time. If the bunkers are driven into a jetty, there might even be a blitz that lasts for some time and provides dream fishing for many anglers over a period of half-an-hour or so. But more common is the quick blast that provides the opportunity to get off only a single, well-placed cast to intercept the fast-moving, blasting bass.

A problem for surfcasters is that beach buggies can't be used on the northern New Jersey beaches where the action is likely to unfold, and parking spots are at a premium during the prime tourist season. The bass are mostly 25- to 40-pounders, with a good shot at a trophy 50-pounder, but anglers spend a lot of time tracking bunker schools along the coast and waiting for the unseen bass to decide it's time for them to make their move.

Even then, there can be frustration, like I encountered once after finally getting in front of a school being pushed tight to me at Long Branch. My cast with a large Yo-Zuri Surface Cruiser was perfect, right into the boiling bass and bunkers. I hooked something immediately, but it felt too small, and it was. I had snagged a bunker, which would have been fine were I fishing a snag hook, though I doubted a striper would hit a bunker with that big plug hanging on it. By the time I reeled the bunker in and released it, the blitz was over, and so was my only opportunity that evening.

Fortunately, I got lucky early the next morning in the same spot. Despite missing the blitz on a bunker school, I ran down to the surf to join the lone angler there who was fighting a bass. I made a desperation cast into the area and drew a blind strike on the big pencil popper and I was able to release a bass well over 30 pounds. I got one other opportunity that morning and was successful in releasing another large striper, making up for a lot of frustration that week.

No matter when or where it occurs, and whatever the size or type of game fish, the thrill of the blitz never diminishes for the surfcaster. Hopefully, you too will enjoy that incomparable experience, which keeps us all coming back day after day in hopes of being there when it happens.

Admire your catch when you can; once the blitz is on, you won't have the time. (Joe Blaze photo)

Surfcasting Strategies

All the information provided in this book won't do any good unless you actually get down to the surf and start putting that knowledge to use. It's fine to understand the theory, but that's no substitute for time on the beach. While most of that time probably won't be productive in terms of fish caught, it could be invaluable in learning what must be done in order to be a successful surfcaster.

Perhaps the most important thing you can do is to make friends in the area you'll be fishing. Most surfcasters are friendly, and quite willing to help those politely asking for information. It's not just what is, or isn't happening now that's important, but also whatever pearls of wisdom can be garnered about what's occurred recently or usually happens at this time of year or under various conditions, plus the techniques involved. Years of experience can be poured out at no cost to those who are good listeners and demonstrate the requisite desire to learn. There's just no substitute for such information, and it's relatively easy to come by.

Joining a local fishing club with lots of surfcasters is another means of getting a leg up that will save lots of trial-and-error. Also patronize tackle shops specializing in surfcasting. Your purchases will bring valuable information from the owners who have a financial interest in your success, and you'll also have another opportunity to mix with anglers who may be of

Rich Rusznak lands a bluefish with classic fly-rod form on a gently sloping beach. (Joe Blaze photo)

help. Never be afraid to ask questions, and don't forget to reciprocate. Should you stumble across something of value, be sure to pass it on to those you're receiving information from or you'll soon see your sources dry up.

Even when nothing much is going on along the beach, productive time can be spent observing the lay of the land at various stages of the tide and under varying weather circumstances. When a run of fish does occur, you'll be much better situated to take advantage of it.

For instance, as noted in the chapter on reading the surf, there are sloughs that will consistently hold fish even though they may be hard to spot on a high tide. Those spots may stand out at low water, and that knowledge could make all the difference at other stages of the tide when they might not be obvious.

Tide is a critical factor when fishing the surf as even small changes in water level can make all the difference. Sand bars that are too shallow on lower tides become a great attraction once covered by enough water, especially so when there's enough wind or high enough seas to produce white water on the bar. The area you ordinarily fish may not have enough water at low tide to hold fish. Yet, there could be another spot not too far away

On steeper beaches, fish without teeth, like this striper, can be landed by grasping them by the lower lip. (Joe Blaze photo)

that features a sharp drop-off and is actually better at low tide because that small deep area tends to concentrate fish. By acquiring this information you can fish various areas at different stages of the tide and maximize your opportunities.

Weather forecasts are important in determining where you focus your efforts. Of course, they're not always right in terms of wind force. However, knowing the wind direction and how high the waves are will be a big help. After a while you'll learn what areas are best on various winds, and whether they're fishable in big seas. Some of the most memorable days on the surf occur during bad weather, but there are also occasions when the water is so discolored or full of weed that there's little hope. These are things you'll have to learn in your area by putting in the time.

Different shorelines call for revised tactics. Here the author works the jetty wash, which corrals bait and makes it vulnerable to feeding fish. (Joe Blaze photo)

Angler uses the action of the waves to work fish toward the beach. (Joe Blaze photo)

Keep a log of your fishing on a daily basis. Over a period of time you'll be able to look back and put together some sort of pattern for particular spots under various conditions. This will help maximize your opportunities to be at the right place at the right time, which is the bottom line in consistently catching fish from the surf.

This is what it's all about: Ristori shows off an early morning striper that his a plug along the jetty at Sea Girt, New Jersey. (Joe Blaze photo)

While there is no substitute for having a network of friends to keep you informed of fish movement, it's also important to follow news reports in local fishing columns and radio or TV shows, where they're available. Just keep in mind that everything you get from those reports is a day old, and much of what happens on the surf is a mere flash in time. There are periods when fishing is good for days, particularly during migrations, but more often the blitz one day will not be repeated the next day, even if conditions remain the same. Nevertheless, that's still your best bet to get into a hot bite and you must be ready to follow it up. Staying in bed and waiting for the call that it's happening again may cost you your best opportunity of the season.

Though most surfcasters dream of being all alone on the beach when the fish of their choice is chasing bait into the wash, other anglers can be a big help in locating fish. I make no bones about the fact that one of my principle methods of locating fish along the surf involves watching for bent rods or anglers walking into the wash to land or release their catch. That's often a more reliable clue than bird activity and bait concentrations.

Indeed, it was a bent rod that put me on fish a few years ago after having suffered a minor stroke. My doctor wouldn't let me drive, but my wife surprised me one morning by offering to drive me to the surf. It was later in the morning than I'd ordinarily leave, and I had no expectations when we pulled up to a favorite street ending in Bay Head on the Jersey Shore. There were only a few birds picking around and no signs of fish, but the lone angler on the beach had a bent rod. I scrambled back to the car, grabbed my rod and a metal lure, and proceeded to release lots of school striped bass by casting blind into surf that showed no signs other than those casually picking birds. I would never have made a cast there if it hadn't been for that single bent rod, but I ended up making my wife late for work because the stripers wouldn't stop hitting, even as the sun got higher in the sky. Fortunately, her boss is a surfcaster and appreciated the fact that I couldn't leave them biting!

Angler body language can also be helpful as just observing concentrations of fishermen, and how hard they're working an area is a clue as to whether something has been going on and might recur. I even check the surfcasters' body language when boat fishing, keeping an eye out for anglers ganging up instead of spreading themselves out along the beach.

While conditions during a storm may be unfishable, the beginning of a storm is one of the best times to be on the beach. Adjustments may have

With the right touch and deft timing on the part of the angler, this striper landed itself on the sand. (Joe Blaze photo)

to be made in terms of heavier tackle in order to cast lures or bait into the wind, but game fish are apt to be feeding close to the wash as the surf is building.

Though the immediate aftermath of a storm may not be the best time to fish the surf, your best opportunity could occur shortly thereafter.

Often stripers will feed very close to the beach in the trough formed by a drop-off in the bottom. Rich Rusznak has presented his fly parallel to the waves so the fly remains in the trough longer. (Joe Blaze photo)

Especially during the spring and fall, storms trigger migrations of bait fish. That, in turn, attracts the game fish that feed on them. It can be frustrating to watch those schools move along without being disturbed, but sooner or later the predators will take their toll and you've got to be patient enough to wait them out.

Storms can also present an opportunity for exceptional bait fishing as shellfish are uprooted and smashed on the beach. That happens along the Jersey Shore when a northeaster creates waves that fill beaches with surf clams. As those clams die, open up, and are washed back into the surf, striped bass feed on them right along the drop-off and become easy targets for anglers who pick up fresh clams at their feet and fish them just yards away from where they're standing.

The timing of your efforts in the surf must be attuned to those of the fish you're seeking. Though most game fish feed both night and day,

Jerry Fabiano takes his time convincing a striper to leave the deeper water beyond the drop-off. (Joe Blaze photo)

some are more active at certain times. The low light periods of dawn and dusk are traditionally the most rewarding for most predators, especially when that time of day coincides with the desired tide and weather conditions. Without knowing a thing about an area I'm fishing for the first time, that's when I'll be trying rather than during the middle of the day or at night.

Bob Noonan fishes Barnegat Inlet because he knows that at dusk predator fish are often feeding heavily. (Joe Blaze photo)

AFTER DARK

Surfcasting at night presents challenges not faced during the day, but can be the most effective way to catch some species under particular conditions. Bait is a most important consideration in determining when to fish. For instance, if predators are feeding on migratory schooling bait that moves during the day, they're not apt to feed actively at night. On the other hand, if bait is scarce during the day, it's likely that predators will be seeking whatever they can find in the dark.

Night fishing is actually quite pleasant under the full moon, and that's usually a good time to try it. The dark of the moon presents more challenges. In some areas, there's a problem with phosphorescence that lights up your lure and makes it look unrealistic. You'll have no problem following it under those circumstances, but when that condition is absent you may find yourself reeling your lures right up to the tip of the rod. Though a long leader with a knot that interferes with your cast is annoying, it can

Sometimes the best strategy is simply being in the right place at the right time. This angler hits pay dirt at dawn. (Alberto Knie photo)

be a help at night, as you feel the knot hit your tiptop and know when to slow the retrieve.

Fishing your lure right to the beach is important during the day as many hits occur right at the drop-off and even more important at night when fish are even less reluctant to strike in just inches of water. Be sure your drag is set light enough to prevent both a break-off and ripping out hooks with a fish thrashing on only a few feet of line. At that point, with the fish hitting so close, you may only have to back up a couple of steps to beach the fish!

Some anglers are very sensitive about lights being shined in the water at night, so it's good form to only point a flashlight toward the beach when removing hooks or changing lures. Actually, most fish are attracted to steady lights at night. Lights from shore-side piers and restaurants, and even street lamps attract bait, and predators tend to hang around the shadow lines. On the other hand, flashes of light might spook them.

Do everything slowly and surely at night. Even simple things, such as completely closing a snap after changing lures, can be fouled up. Shuffle your feet while wading in order not to step into a hole or over a drop-off; and, in tropical areas, shuffle to stir up rays before they remind with their barb you that you have stepped on them. Check landmarks as you walk onto a beach, and plan your return.

It's very easy to get confused after dark, especially if you've been walking up and down the surfline.

While most of us are happy to have our feet solidly planted in the sand, there are some venturesome anglers who extend their range by wearing wet suits. That's become quite common at Montauk Point. Long Island's eastern tip on the south side features many boulders close to shore, and wet suit anglers swim out to them for a perch that puts them tight among the striped bass they seek. Needless to say, only strong swimmers should attempt that extreme fishing which also requires the finest reels that will stand up to being completely submerged.

Landscape and hazards of Montauk take on a different dimension once the sun goes down. Know the area you are fishing and move carefully when fishing after dark. (Alberto Knie photo)

CHAPTER 12

Extreme Surfcasting

The surface-swimming plug drifted out to sea in the current of the roaring river mouth after an easy 100-foot cast from shore. I was ankle deep in the water a few feet from the tropical shore, watching the plug undulate every time I pulled against the taut line. Then there was a huge swirl as the lure disappeared where a silvery shape had flashed. It didn't take long to identify the fish as an 80-pound-class tarpon, since it exploded into the air as soon as it felt the sting of those treble hooks.

The silver king had all the advantages with the current flowing out to the Caribbean, which is where he was headed. It seemed impossible that the fish could be turned on 20-pound spinning tackle. Yet, after more head-shaking jumps, the tarpon was not only stopped before stripping the medium-sized spinning reel, but actually responded to the pressure and moved back to the river mouth. Ten more minutes and I was able to lead him inside the narrow opening. Once he was out of the main current, I had a much better chance of controlling him. There were more jumps, but much weaker ones than those at the beginning of the fight. The tarpon tried to get back in the main flow and out to sea, but I put as much pressure on him as I dared to prevent that. As I had learned by sad experience, a tired tarpon going back to sea while constrained by the efforts of the angler is an easy meal for voracious sharks. Finally, the tired fish moved out

Joe Brooks battles demanding conditions with conventional tackle in this classic photo. Heavy surf and a big ocean provide plenty of close-to-home challenges for the serious surfcaster. (courtesy IGFA)

of the river mouth and into the quiet water behind it before I slid him just high enough up on the sandy shore to remove the plug from his jaw.

I then eased the silver king back in the water and worked him back and forth until he was ready to swim away.

COSTA RICAN ADVENTURES

Many of the species caught regularly by surfcasters are quite large, but the average surf angler will never experience the thrill of catching such large game fish as those I tangled with many years ago at the mouth of Costa Rica's Parismina River, just a short walk from the lodge at Parismina Tarpon Rancho. I caught those tarpon early in the morning before breakfast, and under the moon at night. Other than the trip when I had my nephew, Bob Correll, with me, no one ever seemed to bother taking that short walk from the camp, even when tarpon fishing was tough from the boats. I did pressure the owner at that time, Jerry Tricomi, to join me at the river mouth one morning to take photos and make a few casts. Surprisingly, there wasn't anything else hitting those surface plugs at night, though I did catch a snook one morning.

This tarpon was taken by the author on heavy baitcasting (musky style) tackle at the mouth of the Parismina River on the east coast of Costa Rica.

The river mouth was so narrow that I first started casting with the same 5-foot baitcasting rod and Ambassadeur 7000 reel that was standard for fishing from the boats, and I was still able to cast almost to the sand on the other side of the river. The tarpon were farther out, where the current met the breakers, but there was no need to cast directly to them. Just getting the plug across was enough to let the current carry it to the rolling tarpon while I free-spooled.

Fortunately, those tarpon were only 60- to 80-pounders, as I might have been in trouble if they'd been the 100-pounders that are caught in the same area some years.

There was no need to get anything but my ankles wet which I realized was just as well when I watched a shark tear apart a hooked tarpon inside the river mouth. I never saw any native swimming in that surf! It would have been easy to get swept off my feet in the strong current, or knocked over by the tree trunks silently floating downriver as I cast with my back to them.

Another day, while despairing of catching a tarpon inshore from one of the small guide boats, my nephew and I went ashore on the other side of the river mouth, where we each caught a tarpon in classic surfcasting fashion as the fish rolled in the waves. It wasn't easy fishing in a rough surf, though the setting was colorful, against the backdrop of a stranded shrimp boat, victim of the nearby revolution in Nicaragua. Jack crevalle were also in the surf, as well as very large snook, especially in late summer and early fall.

HOMEBOY TARPON

Those earlier shorebound tussles with tarpon led me to my favorite shore fishing in the Florida Keys. That involves using surf-spinning gear to cast from the sides of bridges. Tarpon are usually found on the up-tide side of the bridges, swimming in front of the pilings to ambush shrimp and small fish drawn out of the Gulf to the ocean on the outgoing tide. Long casts usually aren't required to reach tarpon that generally are in the 30- to 60-pound class, but it takes a lot of drag to stop the hooked fish from running with the current and under the bridge. Surprisingly, some tarpon head up-tide after jumping, and give the angler a chance to get them out of harm's way. The occasional much larger tarpon always seems to wise up in time and turn with the current to swim through the bridge and end the battle.

Just as I found with the river mouth tarpon, additional pressure applied in a particular direction often steers big fish where you want them to go. Apply maximum pressure with the rod low and pointed in the opposite direction the fish is running, and you'll often be able to steer him away from obstacles or turn him in a better direction.

Though a wide variety of plugs and jigs will draw hits, I prefer the DOA Baitbuster in the deep-running version as it's consistently effective and the single hook is easier and safer to remove on those occasions when a tarpon is fought to shore. The Tsunami shad jig is another good choice.

Capt. Charlie Fornabio, a guide at Sebastian, Florida, has developed methods of catching large tarpon from the surf in his area. He's estimated his releases of tarpon up to 80 inches, with a 50-inch girth, at 135 to 140 pounds. Fornabio grew up along the New Jersey coast and became an expert at catching big striped bass in the surf. Though he's busy guiding anglers to snook, red drum, tarpon, spotted sea trout, and other species from his boat, Fornabio treasures his free time in the fall when mullet runs along the shore attract tarpon into the surf. The prime time is from the second week in September to early November, all along the coast from Jensen Beach up to St. Augustine. The first three weeks of October are usually best, with that third week normally the peak. A low incoming tide is favored, especially at dawn and dusk, as the trough is filling in. Calm weather may be pretty, but it's not good for the tarpon fishery. Just as with striper fishing, Fornabio looks for an onshore wind creating white water. Indeed, rough seas are best. Four anglers once jumped over 100 tarpon at the south jetty of Sebastian Inlet during a storm in the second week of November.

Fornabio uses heavy spinning tackle (a 10-foot custom rod with a Van Staal 250 reel filled with 30-pound Suffix braided line) and favors that old big-striper favorite, the Atom 40, though the treble hooks are switched to much heavier Owner trebles. Chartreuse is the favored color, and Fornabio also sprays white plugs with fluorescent gold paint. The large plug is worked very slowly, and Fornabio turns the eye up slightly so it digs in a bit to prevent tumbling in the waves. He also casts a 3-ounce Super Strike popper that he swims as well as pops. That lure casts better into the wind, and also attracts blacktip and spinner sharks. The swimmer is a better bet for an occasional big red drum or barracuda, and 5- to 15-pound snook in the trough. Though the best bet is casting to rolling tarpon, many of Fornabio's tarpon hits come while blind casting in the trough.

Capt. Charlie Fornabio hoists a bruiser tarpon from the surf at Sebastian, Florida. (Charlie Fornabio photo)

The leader is 80- to 100-pound fluorocarbon with a custom sailfish snap made with marlin wire. This not only provides some protection against the tarpon's raspy mouth, but also has the breaking strength required when landing such a large fish. A big surf helps in the landing process by lifting the fish onto the beach.

Fornabio's surf tarpon tactics often result in untargeted heavyweight catches. Here he avoids the business end of a sizeable blacktip shark. (Charlie Fornabio photo)

FARTHER AFIELD

When the quarry is large and challenging, fishing from a sand beach is a great comfort compared to what anglers in some other parts of the world have to go through in order to catch large fish from shore. In places such as South Africa and Hawaii, fishermen often venture out on dangerous cliffs to cast to a variety of large fish, a daunting list that at times even includes giant pelagic species such as tuna.

In his book *Strike* (A.A. Balkema, Cape Town, 1982) S. Schoeman notes that December 28, 1945, was a red letter day in the annals of South African rock angling because a party of six anglers landed twenty one bluefin tuna from the rocks at Rooikrantz, Cape Point, and lost many more.

Those tuna were under 30 pounds though giants were also hooked. A tuna club was soon formed as anglers from all over South Africa rushed to the scene, and in the next month the *Cape Times* reported:

"Scenes unprecedented in the annals of False Bay angling were witnessed at Rooikrantz on Saturday when hundreds of tunny ran wild and shoals of flying fish soared through the air in all directions in an effort to escape from the big fish chasing them. A party of six Cape Town anglers landed a total of 22, the biggest of which scaled 16 kg and the smallest 11 kg. Between 40 and 50 more tunny were hooked but broke away. Of the total of 22 caught, 19 were bluefin tunny and 3 were yellowfin tunny, a rare species, one of which was sent to the South African Museum, Cape Town. The tunny were fighting mad. They churned up the sea in seething, massed rushes. Time and again, 3.5m giants, some of them 2m in girth and scaling almost 450 kg were hooked and fought savagely for five or six minutes before breaking away. At one stage three of the huge fish were being played at the same time. Wriggling, snapping and leaping high into the air, they presented a wonderful spectacle in their efforts to tear away from the hooks. . . . At intervals hundreds of tunny were seen charging at shoals of flying fish that broke surface and leaped high in the air to escape their voracious enemy."

Though South African rock anglers were amazed at that display, digging though old records revealed that a 75.04-kilogram tuna had been landed in January 1932 by a member of the South Breakwater Fishing Club of Port Elizabeth, and another angler had caught a 79.37-kilogram tuna at South Pier, Durban. The bluefin runs petered out while yellowfin became

Anglers have many challenges fishing the Cape of Good Hope, South Africa, but with deep water sweeping inshore, tuna are always a possibility.

more common catches from the rocks, culminating with the landing of a 70.75-kilogram yellowfin at Rooikrantz on May 6, 1956, in under two hours, and a 70.8-kilogram at the Bull's Nose, Simonstown. Considering the tackle and accessories available at the time, it was remarkable that shore anglers were able to make such catches.

While tuna rarely come within range of surfcasters, sick or injured oceanic species very occasionally end up close to shore. That's what happened during the fall of 1996 off Deal, New Jersey. Veteran boat striper fisherman Big Al Wutkowski was casting from his Flume into the jetties, along with his partner, Capt. Bruce Alesso, when he spotted a surfcaster continually casting at big swirls behind a pair of "T" jetties. The angler finally hooked up, but Wutkowski noticed that the fish wasn't fighting like a big striper. Instead, it raced around the lagoon-like waters between the jetties before tiring out. At that point, Wutkowski saw that it was snagged in the back with a black Bomber swimming plug. Eventually, he was able to throw a rope to the beach fisherman and tie the other end to the exhausted tuna's tail after gaffing it for him. At 53 inches, the bluefin was estimated at about 125 pounds—quite a catch from shore on 20-pound line, though hardly up to IGFA standards.

At that point, Wutkowski realized the bluefin season was closed and he couldn't legally put it in his boat. He told the angler it would have to be his responsibility to deal with the tuna. The surfcaster was able to borrow a wheelbarrow from a contractor working nearby, and got his catch off the beach.

Ironically, as difficult as it is to catch an oceanic tuna from shore along the United States Atlantic coast, it's not legal to keep one as a pelagic species permit is required—and they're only issued to boats, not fishermen. At the time of the catch described, there was only a bluefin tuna permit involved. Since then regulation has been expanded to include all the tunas, except the inshore little tunny, plus pelagic sharks and billfish. It's unlikely that the National Marine Fisheries Service would pursue the issue in such rare cases, but surfcasters might be reluctant to brag about their great catch upon learning that it's technically illegal.

Sharks are also fair game for surf and jetty specialists. Once again, the South Africans have established some incredible standards. Schoeman noted that Bill Selkirk landed a shark of 986.98 kilograms from the rocks at Hermanus on rod and reel, but didn't specify the species. Reg Harrison of Durban landed a blue pointer (great white) of 752.7 kilograms in July 1953, and another angler caught a 468.79-kilogram tiger shark from South Pier, Durban.

Some Americans are also dedicated to catching big sharks from shore. That's particularly the case in Florida and at Cape Hatteras. I once saw a truck at Hatteras backed up to the surf with a fighting chair bolted to the cargo bed and big-game tackle brought into play as shark baits floated out over the bar under balloons or kites. When the wind isn't favorable and the surf not too high, some anglers have even rowed the baits out in small boats. That big sharks come close to shore should be no surprise, as the long-standing IGFA all-tackle world record tiger shark was taken from the pier at Cherry Grove, South Carolina, by Walter Maxwell on June 14, 1964.

Other surfcasters fishing with bait hook sharks unintentionally, and some actually end up landing them despite a lack of wire leader, if the hook sets in the corner of the shark's mouth. That's especially the case now with many bait fishermen using circle hooks. The shark's close cousin, the ray,

Surf fishing, even close to home, can be as extreme as you want to make it. This Pennsylvania angler has mounted a fighting chair in the bed of his pickup to accommodate the heavy offshore tackle he uses to land big sharks from the surf at Cape Hatteras.

The author with a ray that struck a metal lure at Bayhead, New Jersey. Though not a targeted species, rays provide a great surf battle.

also provides a thrill to anglers who think they've hooked the red drum or striped bass of their dreams.

The cownose ray is a strong and fast opponent that will make long runs—and frequently hits lures as well as bait. While skates are actually desired by European anglers, no one fishes for them in the United States.

CHAPTER 13

Surfcasting Pioneers

and Classics

Surfcasting has attracted some of the great names in fishing, among them many who were much better known for their big game exploits. A hero of mine as a youth was S. Kip Farrington, Jr., a wealthy angler who explored big game fishing throughout the world, but also enjoyed surfcasting on Long Island. Over and over I read every word in Farrington's classic, *Fishing the Atlantic, Offshore and On* (Coward-McCann, Inc., New York, 1949) as I grew up in the 1950s. While his exploits with giant tuna and billfish might as well have been in another world, I could relate to his accounts of surf fishing.

Fishing tackle was still relatively primitive in those post-WWII years. Farrington cited the 1947 Census of Manufacturers that included 2,184,000 wood and bamboo fishing rods, and 954,000 metal fishing rods, though there was no mention of fiberglass rods as yet. Servicemen returning from Europe would soon be introducing spinning and monofilament lines to America, but Farrington was casting at Montauk with the best equipment then available—a Penn Squidder and 9-thread linen line that was "hot" under the thumb and had to be washed in fresh water and dried after each use. Metal squids were the lures he cast for striped bass, and since there was no monofilament for leaders, Farrington used No. 7 to No. 9 piano wire, even though stripers have no cutting teeth. Modern anglers

Joe Brooks and Frank Woolner, writing from their own pioneering efforts, brought the excitement of surfcasting to thousands of anglers. (Dick Woolner photo, courtesy IGFA)

are reluctant to use wire leaders even for sharp-toothed species as they interfere with lure action.

Every cast was an adventure in those days, and Farrington noted, "Don't worry about backlashing. Everybody gets them and everybody breaks off jigs. Don't forget to wet your line on the spool with a few hand-fuls of water before casting. And don't try to cast too far until your line is thoroughly wet."

Farrington mentioned the possibility of catching pollock from the Montauk surf in the spring, something that hasn't happened now for many decades.

Farrington also fished from shore in Rhode Island, where he found "almost constant action" with striped bass except for two or three lean weeks toward the end of July.

> *"It is nearly all early-morning and late-evening fishing. The tide does not seem to make a great deal of difference, and my guess would be that water conditions are almost always ideal except right after a hard easterly blow. The water is never too clear with any wind condition, which seems to make the bass strike better in that locality, and the surf man will find the highly-thought-of champagne water on many tides.*
>
> *"Most of the angling is practiced from high cliffs, with the surf breaking some distance below. You almost always can find good footing to cast from, and the height contributes to the ease of making a good cast. The only difficulty is that you have to run down the cliff to grab your fish. This little trick is not as easy as it sounds, but it adds to the variety of the sport, as you have to pick your spot, and climbing down in the darkness adds a little zest—at least it does for me.*
>
> *"Here I would venture to say that seventy percent of the striped bass are taken on plugs, twenty percent on eel skins, and ten percent on lead squids. There is practically no bait fishing."*

Farrington noted that some of the Narragansett fishermen chum bass to the rocks with pieces of menhaden, and may do so for two or three tides, though "this method of enticement is frowned upon by most members of the fraternity," he noted. At least their chumming with menhaden (pogies, bunkers) was a lot cheaper than with the lobsters that were favored during the previous century by Cuttyhunk, Massachusetts, guides to attract stripers

Taking the sport beyond the familiar, Joe Brooks explored the world. Here he fishes the Bermuda surf for gafftopsail pompano. (courtesy IGFA)

to the casting stands of the Cuttyhunk Club (1865 to 1907) constructed among the rocks there for the benefit of wealthy visiting anglers.

Farrington goes on to note that, "Strange as it may seem, you do not have to make a long cast. I know of no place where stripers are taken on a shorter cast. The water is deep right up to the base of the ledge that you are standing on, and you constantly will be seeing fish swimming up behind your lures and looking them over. It is practically all spot casting, and it is highly desirable to put your plug exactly where you want it over and around certain rocks. The ideal spots are holes and indentures in the rocky coastline."

Farrington cited Narragansett tackle shop owner Jerry Sylvester as "one of the country's finest surf fishermen as well as one of the most ardent students of striped bass I have ever known." That praise was well deserved, as Sylvester had broken Farrington's world record for stripers on 6-thread (18-pound-test line) with a 57-pounder. Another angler many years ago told me Sylvester knew every underwater rock so well that he would bet other anglers he could catch a bass with a single cast after they'd already taken their casts. He would then lay his cast right into the white water just as a wave broke on the rock and win the bet every time. Sylvester also urged Farrington to slow his retrieve as stripers seldom care to chase their prey. They want a crippled fish that's imitated with a slow retrieve.

Farrington didn't ignore the surf during his overseas trips to explore big game possibilities. It was the promise of 1,000-pound black marlin that drew him to Cabo Blanco, Peru. While there, on September 11, 1952, he took the day off from big game trolling to go surfcasting after Sunday mass. He noted in *Fishing the Pacific, Offshore and On* (Coward-McCann, New York, 1953) that, "I had marvelous luck, catching a 17-pound snook on my fourth cast with a lead jig. Later I took another, and was well satisfied with the day."

Farrington was a great fan of the roosterfish, but it seems he was never fortunate enough to catch one from the surf. In discussing experiences in Ecuador, Farrington stated:

"On 6- and 9-thread line the roosterfish gives a fine account of himself—particularly on the former. The fight is up to anything one can get out of an amberjack with a dolphin thrown in. Usually there are four or five good jumps and sometimes this fish will make magnificent runs on the surface with his beautiful dorsal fin raised high

like a rooster's comb. He is a real scrapper and of all the game fish in the Pacific I would rate this one tenth as far as fighting potential is concerned. He ranks just after the dolphin in my estimation. To catch roosterfish playing around and feeding off the beach is a thrilling experience. I can hardly wait until I take one surfcasting. This year (1953) Gardiner Marsh, the great Atlantic caster from Nantucket, took them at Cabo San Lucas up to 48 pounds, and he considered that in all his casting experience they were the greatest fish he has ever taken with a surf rod. They really go to town when hooked. Unfortunately, I didn't spend enough time surfcasting in Peru. Otherwise I might have been lucky enough to land one of these beauties."

In his section on California, Farrington detailed the incredible proliferation of the striped bass from the relatively few fingerlings that crossed the country by railroad in 1879. Just 107 stripers, mostly 1 to 3 inches in length, were shipped from the Navesink River in New Jersey and liberated in the Carquinez Straits near San Francisco. An additional 300 were shipped from the Shrewsbury River in New Jersey in 1882, and released in Suisun Bay, California. From those insignificant stockings, the Pacific Coast striper population became established. A 17-pounder was caught four years after their West Coast introduction, and a 45-pounder after 10 years. In 1915, an 87-pounder was netted in Suisun Bay. Striped bass became so popular with California anglers that they were declared a game fish there in 1935, long before such action was taken on the East Coast.

Farrington only mentioned San Francisco striped bass surf fishing in passing, noting that Baker's Beach, in the very shadow of the Golden Gate Bridge, is one of the most popular places to fish, but he regretted that bait fishing was the preferred tactic. "Unfortunately there is not much squidding with metal jigs on the California coast and the bass do not seem to hit them with any regularity," he lamented. He also mentioned that "Surf anglers south of San Luis Obispo also are having magnificent sport with the yellowtail, which fights harder in the surf than the striped bass. And there are three other excellent species: the spotfin croaker, the yellowfin croaker, and the corbina." Though big game was his passion, Farrington also praised those relatively small fish, plus others that could be caught from the surf on bait—such as greenling, rockfish, mackerel, and sea perch.

Chisie Farrington accompanied her husband on many of his fishing adventures, and became a great angler in her own right with her own big game world records. She also wrote a book, *Women Can Fish, Salt Water,*

Pete Connell with skinny 51.5-inch striper caught casting an eel at evening from a New Jersey jetty. (Allen Riley Photo)

Surf and Fresh Water (Coward-McCann, Inc., New York, 1951). When there were no boats, nor gasoline available to run them for sport-fishing during WWII, the Farringtons were grounded, and Chisie also became a surf-caster. She came to love the sport. "At first the line would land in a bunch at my feet, then it would go out a few yards but never out straight and never where I wanted to put it." Though she developed a fair cast without too many backlashes, Chisie conceded, "I don't really expect to catch anything when I am casting from the beach."

Van Campen Heilner was another aristocratic angler from Long Island who specialized in big game, but also loved surfcasting. His *Salt Water*

Fishing (Alfred A. Knopf, New York, 1946) was another bible of mine as a teenager. Channel bass (now called red drum) were Heilner's surfcasting specialty, and he fished for them from Barnegat Light, New Jersey, to the Gulf of Mexico. As he noted:

> *"Surf fishing is to saltwater angling what trout fishing is to fresh water. It is a one-man game from start to finish. You are the one and only factor.*
>
> *"If he runs out all the line you can't pick up oars or start the engine and follow him. No cushion or comfortable chair supports your fundament, no thwarts against which to brace your feet, no companion to assist you or guide you. You must find your quarry yourself, you must rig and bait your hook yourself, you must become proficient in the art of casting so you can reach him, and you must bring him through the line of foaming breakers and surging tides until at last, whipped to a standstill, he lies gasping at your very feet. Then you must let him go because he deserves it."*

Heilner cited his friend and famed big game angler, Phillip Mayer, whom he judged to be the most dedicated channel bass angler on the coast. Mayer kept a diary of all his channel bass catches, and had a total of 7,422 by November 7, 1936, topped by 761 in 1933. Yet, Mayer complained that of all those channel bass, "I doubt if there were 30 fish that would exceed 50 pounds each." Fortunately, Mayer was a conservationist at a time when almost all fish were killed, and he kept only those that swallowed hooks, releasing "fully 80% of all fish caught." Many of the areas fished at that time (such as Corsons and Barnegat inlets in New Jersey) haven't produced adult red drum in decades. Even the young (referred to as puppy drum) are rare.

When it came to channel bass, there were few anglers better at the sport than Claude Rogers of Virginia. Famed outdoor writer Vlad Evanoff profiled Rogers in his *Fishing Secrets of the Experts* (Doubleday & Co., Garden City, New York, 1962). Rogers stated:

> *"The channel bass is king of the Southern surf and one of the great blessings for the East Coast angler. His size, his range, his co-operative feeding habits, the manner in which he may be taken make him available to the expert and amateur angler alike.*
>
> *"He may be taken at different seasons from piers, surf, and boat. He accepts bait, cut and live, lures, cast or trolled, and all in all, he is most cooperative, if given*

a chance. But the sportiest way to take old Sciaenops ocellatus *is from the surf and no dyed-in-the-wool surfcaster considers his life complete if he has not had the opportunity to catch both channel bass and striped bass and compare the fighting qualities of each."*

A photo shows Rogers with channel bass of 48 and 53 pounds taken during the fall from the surf at Cobbs Island, Virginia. Rogers was one of the surfcasting pioneers along the Virginia barrier islands that could only be accessed by small boat.

Rogers preferred fish heads for channel bass bait. He emphasized that conditions often dictate the choice of bait—particularly durability.

"There are times when a strong current makes it difficult for the surfcaster or pier fisherman to hold bottom regardless of what size and shape of sinker he employs. At such times it is necessary, once the sinker does take hold, that the bait be durable enough to resist the chewing efforts of all the little crabs in the area for a reasonable length of time and maintain an attractive appearance to the first jumbo channel bass that appears.

"Actually, these little animated chum grinders are one of the angler's mixed blessings, for while a little calico crab is busily chewing away at the fish head, he is also creating a small and attractive "slick" for the game fish the angler seeks. On the other hand, a big blue crab can chew away a slab of cut bait so rapidly that the angler is forced to waste precious time with frequent bait changes and re-anchoring the sinker in the fast currents. The most durable bait available locally, and suffi-ciently oily to be attractive to fish in thick (sandy) water is the head with a portion of the body trimmed from a 6-inch mullet or spot.

"To rig this type of bait simply force the hook up through the lower jaw and out through the nose, exposing the entire point of the hook. The hard, bony blue crab is a principle item of food for the channel bass, so the bass is not likely to spot the hook simply because a portion of the barb is exposed. Menhaden, though quite oily and ideal for cut bait, is unsuited for this chore as the frail, bony head contains little flesh and tears from the hook quite easily."

Rogers, were he still on the scene, just might not be surprised to know that bunker heads are still, to this day, the preferred bait of surfcasters seek-ing trophy bass. As well, his preferred rigging of terminal tackle, in the breakaway rig, seems to have stood the test of time.

Tom Fote landing large striper in Island Beach State Park surf. As legislative director of the Jersey Coast Anglers Association, Fote was a determining voice in earning game fish status for striped bass in New Jersey.

"Some of my angler friends say that fish heads are also attractive to shark and other pests, but as long as the bait is 'attractive' I will put up with the inconvenience of a few sharks. I use hooks snelled with a 60-pound monofilament since the monofilament acts as a 'releasing link' and you do not waste valuable fishing time fighting sharks.

"The use of fish heads for bait, although desirable under the conditions just described, makes casting somewhat bulky and difficult. There are times when maximum distance is the condition essential to success. Quite often this is the case when fishing the area of Cape Hatteras known as the 'Point.' Here, during the fall months, channel bass will congregate off this underwater peninsula, formed by opposing currents, where the seas toss together in a peculiar manner that provides a marine banquet table for Mr. Red Drum. Only those anglers who can cast to the outer edge of this little underwater spit are successful. Here it is necessary that anglers cut, trim, and rig a streamlined bait of minimum wind resistance. A bait cut in a triangular or pennant shape may be folded at the blunt end and impaled on the hook in such a manner that it is of little bulk and the streamer shape offers little resistance when cast."

Rogers further comments on the importance of reading the water and the bottom contour in order to successfully locate the productive, fish-holding portions of the shoreline. It is advice that still holds value for today's surfcaster:

"Successful surf fishing for channel bass in Virginia and North Carolina generally hinges on the selection of the right slough. These deep water indentations along the shoreline can be recognized by the darker color of the water, if the water is clear. If the slough cannot be identified by the darker shade of the water, then look for an area where incoming waves are not as high as in the surrounding area. Seas tend to build up over shallow areas and level off over deeper holes. And if the sea is dead calm, and sandy, which is rare, look for a telltale eddy that seems to be running directly offshore. Local commercial fishermen call these eddies 'out sucks,' which is pretty descriptive, as they not only carry water out, but any helpless bait fish that are caught up in them. If you are fortunate enough to find a deep slough up against the beach with one of these so-called 'out-sucks' running through a bar that parallels the beach within casting stance, you have it made."

Vlad Evanoff was a noted surf fishermen in his own right. His basic advice was to fish hard and often, and his philosophical approach to the sport rings as true today as when he originally penned it:

> *"Surf fishing is never easy. True there may be bonanza days, when the fish are thick and you can get one on almost every cast. But such days are pretty rare. Most of the time you have to make hundreds, if not thousands, of casts for a few fish. And when it comes to the big fish, many are hooked, but not all of them are landed. Fighting and landing a big striped bass, channel bass, bluefish or weakfish in the surf is difficult and the odds are in favor of the fish. But when you do finally beach a trophy-size fish you can take a bow and feel you've really accomplished something in the fishing world. One big fish from the surf is equal to a dozen of the same size from a boat."*

CHAPTER 14

A World of Surf and

Shore Casting

Though boat fishermen have a big advantage when it comes to catching fish, anglers casting into the surf or from other shore locations can take advantage of a world of opportunities. It's possible to fish day and night most of the year for some species of interest almost anywhere we live or travel near saltwater shores.

In addition to such domestic locations as Maine, Cape Cod and Newburyport, Rhode Island, Block Island, Long Island, the Jersey Shore, Delaware, Ocean City, Virginia Beach, North Carolina's Outer Banks and Ocracoke Island, and both coasts of Florida, I've walked shorelines from South Africa to Australia while casting lures for whatever might hit them. Though not always successful, those hours were memorable and well-spent. From pink salmon on the tidal flats of Sitka, Alaska, to tarpon at the mouth of Costa Rica's Parismina River, it's all been an adventure that supplemented or, in some cases, was better than the boat fishing I traveled for.

As good as the daytime boat fishing may be wherever I travel, I always seek out shore fishing opportunities while others are enjoying their cocktails. After dinner I may be out there again. It's not that I expect anything exceptional when compared to what's being caught during the day, but I find great personal reward in discovering something on my own.

Jim Filip surf fly-fishing at the Korean Wreck on Christmas Island in the South Pacific. (Joe Blaze photo)

That was the case a few years ago when early one morning I walked down the road to the surf from my hotel while sailfishing in Quepos, Costa Rica. Without a clue as to what might be available, I cast a Yo-Zuri Surface Cruiser (pencil popper) hoping for a roosterfish or jack. I was able to wade out far enough to cast over the breakers with a 9-foot, 2-piece surf spinning outfit, and eventually got an impressive surface strike. After a brief battle, I was surprised to slide a cubera snapper onto the beach. To be sure, it wasn't one of the 25- to 50-pounders I love to cast poppers for over structure off tropical eastern Pacific shores. Yet there was a greater sense of accomplishment because of where and how I caught that 14-pounder as I released it to fight another day.

Looking back on many overseas trips over the years, I remember catching snappers from the rocks at Punta Carnero, Ecuador, and a small roosterfish from the surf; jack crevalle from the beach at Cabo San Lucas,

Pete Perinchief and Joe Brooks explore the untapped Bermuda surf with spin and fly tackle in this classic photo. (courtesy IGFA)

Baja California; and jack crevalle, bluefin trevally, and houndfish from the rocks on Isla Coiba, Panama, plus jumping a big spinner shark from the cove on the backside of Club Pacifico de Panama—where I also waded across to a tiny island at low tide and hooked a roosterfish on light tackle.

After that club closed, we had to fish the area from motherships. I was able to get evening rides ashore from the *Coiba Explorer* (before it went out

The author with an unusual surf catch at Quepos Costa Rica—a cubera snapper on a pencil popper.

of business) in an inflatable boat to the small island of Rancheria across from the old camp, where I plugged the shoreline for the same species and the occasional small cubera while hoping for a roosterfish. While roosterfish can be fought from the rocks, a large cubera would have to be exceptionally dumb to be caught in that fashion as the rocks you have to guide him through offer ample opportunity for him to escape. Big cubera are tough enough from a boat, and the only chance you have of landing them is when you screw down the drag to get him away from shore and those rocks.

Now we fish the Coiba area from the Pesca Panama houseboat operation, and daytime shore fishing for snook has been developed on a bay where a stream flows in. We have to keep an eye on the crocodile that shares the beach, but impressive black snook to over 30 pounds live there along with jack crevalle, bluefin trevally, and small snappers. There were no catches during my brief surf attempts in Australia, New Zealand, and on Christmas Island—but I'll get them the next time!

The most unusual surf fishing I ever did was on a remote beach outside a river mouth on the Miskito Coast of Honduras. After flying into

Guide hoists a tarpon the author took from the surf on light spinning tackle from a Costa Rica beach.

Angler plies the surf off the coast of Honduras in Central America. Foreign destinations that specialize in other types of fishing often offer unadvertised surf fishing as a bonus for anglers who are willing to seek it out.

a dirt landing strip in the middle of nowhere, there was further travel by foot, a small boat across a lagoon, on foot along the beach, and finally by canoe across the narrow river to a primitive outpost trading with the Indians. A strong, and surprisingly cool, north wind over the Caribbean that winter made for uncomfortable night conditions as I waded into the rough surf in a bathing suit to cast for snook. The big snook I'd come for were missing, but there were some smaller ones, plus tarpon that hit the same plugs—along with the only Atlantic cubera snapper I've ever caught.

A bonfire on the beach provided some light during the pitch-black nights, and a place to warm up! Average-sized snook could be seen swimming through breakers on the bars during the day in a rough surf, when the wind and waves felt good in the tropical heat.

It's a lot easier at home along the Jersey Shore to stumble out of bed in the morning and make a short drive to the beach for an hour or two of casting and good exercise. The species aren't as exotic, but they're somewhat more dependable—and the breakfast eggs are from chickens rather than iguanas!

Guide gaffing a snook from the surf near the mouth of the San Juan River in Nicaragua.

Surfcasting in New Zealand.

Fishing off the rock cliffs in Korea. Wherever the ocean meets the shore, fishermen are drawn to the surf, as sure as the game fish follow the schools of bait.

CHAPTER 15

Toward the Future:

The Considerate Surfcaster

The joy of surfcasting can have many different meanings, depending on the individual. Some revel in the solitude of the beach, while others view it as an opportunity to socialize with fellow anglers who enjoy the sport. There are no rights and wrongs about those attitudes, and all should be respected. I've found over the years that even those who seemingly most desire their privacy are often quite willing to pour out a mountain of information when properly approached.

There's a fine line between interfering and socializing in what is, after all, a public setting. No one "owns" a particular jetty or slough, but it's a matter of common courtesy not to crowd those who were working a stretch of beach before you arrive.

It's a little different when the bite is on.

When birds are diving and fish are breaking, it's every man for himself. Even the most private surfcaster expects to be crowded when the blitz is on, but good long-term relations dictate providing some elbow room for others even under those circumstances.

Most importantly, look before you leap and don't cast over the line of an angler fighting a fish. Remember that lines cast straight out don't necessarily come in the same way. The effect of wind, waves and current may wash your lure ashore many yards down the beach, where it constitutes a

Solitary days on a deserted stretch of beach are increasingly harder to find. More demand on a finite resource requires courtesy and cooperation among anglers.

These fly anglers must check behind them every time they cast because beach walkers may not be aware of the extent of the backcast of a fly-fisher. (Joe Blaze photo)

There is plenty of room on this jetty to provide space for these anglers. (Joe Blaze photo)

hazard to other anglers wading in the surf. Be very much aware of that before you get excited and snag another surfcaster in the leg or boots at the end of your retrieve.

The same consideration should apply when you are fighting a fish. Move with your fish in an effort to keep it in front of you, rather than allowing your line to stretch down the beach, where it will cut off other anglers' access to the surf. This applies even though you may be literally pushing others out of their spots in order to get through. The unwritten law is that the hooked-up angler has the right-of-way.

There's no rule on how much space to give another angler on the beach. It's basically a matter of common sense to provide enough room for safe casting and fighting fish. The farther away you can be while still being able to cast into fish or productive water, the better.

We often kid about "mugging" anglers who are into fish, but that's the name of the game in the surf, as everyone realizes it's necessary to get hooked up during the often-short periods when fish are available. By working together, everyone's catch will be maximized.

While those hot bites are all too rare for surfcasters, it's important not to get so excited that fish are wasted. The thrill of the catch doesn't necessarily have to end with a kill.

The bad old days of stacking up every legal fish on the beach are fading. Unfortunately, there are still those occasions during a blitz when some

Releasing a bluefish is a two-handed job for this young angler. (Joe Blaze photo)

Properly releasing fish is an important aspect of conservation, sportsmanship, and appreciation of our sport. (Joe Blaze photo)

fishermen throw every fish up on the sand without really knowing what they're going to do with them. Measuring your catch and, perhaps, taking a photo before releasing it is more common today, as peer pressure discourages overkill. There's never any excuse for waste, and surfcasters in general get a bad reputation when fish are left on a beach to rot and draw flies.

Not only should all fish not desired for food be released, but they should be returned in a responsible manner in order to assist in their survival. The practice of kicking fish back into the surf is not acceptable, and can also be dangerous in the case of striped bass, which have sharp dorsal spines quite capable of going right through a boot. It's acceptable to nudge a fish back into the suds with a booted foot if it's come off the hook in the surf, or has been washed back in by waves. The best bet is to release fish on the spot in the wash.

Rich Rusznak about to release a school striper. Fly-fisherman know that for safety glasses should always be worn when fly-casting to protect the eyes from an accident. (Joe Blaze photo)

Those fish that you drag up on the sand should be carried back toward the drop and released into that deeper water where it will be easier for them to overcome wave action until they regain their equilibrium. Those that are particularly tired may have to be worked back and forth to facilitate water flow over the gills before release. Wherever possible, get a handhold at the base of the tail and wait for the fish to shake before sending him on his way. Though that's a safe place to hold most fish, it's not advised without gloves for jacks that have scutes at the base of their tail. Working the fish with the hand under the belly is also effective, but be sure to keep your hands out of the gills. Fish bleeding from the mouth are good candidates for survival, but those bleeding from the gills are in trouble. Fish without teeth, such as striped bass, can safely be handled with a firm lip hold.

It should go without saying that nothing may be left on the beach. Lure fishermen normally carry everything they use on and off in a lure bag, but those fishing with bait must be sure to leave no trace of their activity.

As good as it gets! Practice, patience, and skill come together when a prize striper hits the beach. The author is about to release a striper over 30 pounds at Long Branch, New Jersey. (Joe Blaze photo)

Even used clam shells should be returned to the water, as remaining scraps and juices can smell and attract flies.

Another common problem on the beach involves staking out rods for bottom fishing. This is particularly a source of contention along prime pompano areas on Florida's east coast. There are some jurisdictions where regulations limit the number of rods per angler in order to give everyone a chance to fish prime areas.

Competitive angling isn't as common from the beach as in boats, but there are some famous contests. The annual Martha's Vineyard Tournament in Massachusetts may be the best-known contest drawing surf fisher-men, but there are others that are less intense and even family-oriented. The Governor's Surf Fishing Tournament at Island Beach State Park in New Jersey, held every year at the beginning of October, is such an event. It draws hundreds of anglers fishing for a variety of species in several divisions.

Youngsters walk away with lots of tackle, and the governor often shows up to give the Governor's Cup to the angler catching the largest fish. Just

Donna Zibelski-Harris practices the rudiments of surf fishing that may well carry her through a lifetime of enjoyment. (Donna Harris photo)

The New Jersey Governor's Surf Fishing Tournament. These participants take advantage of balloon-tired chairs for disabled access at Island Beach State Park, New Jersey. Surf fishing is for everyone!

south of there along the Jersey Shore, the Long Beach Island Surf Fishing Tournament is contested for bluefish and striped bass from mid-October to mid-November every year. Beach buggy associations and fishing clubs also hold tournaments, often involving bottom fishing in designated spots along the beach.

Surf-Fishing Meccas in the United States

While surfcasting is possible just about anywhere saltwater meets the shore, there are a few areas that dedicated surfcasters dream of fishing.

THE OUTER BANKS OF NORTH CAROLINA

Cape Hatteras is world famous for its surfcasting. It's probably most associated with red drum, but late fall runs of jumbo bluefish provide greater volume, and big striped bass are baited during the winter. Those who don't want to participate in the shoulder-to-shoulder fishery at The Point can take the ferry across to Ocracoke Island where there's plenty of elbow room. The mouth of Oregon Inlet is another favored area for the same species, and the Outer Banks also produce fine light tackle surf sport in the summer for pompano, and in the fall for spotted sea trout. Red drum are caught primarily on bait fished at night. A few surf specialists also fish for large sharks at Hatteras by sending big baits beyond the outer bar with balloons.

THE JERSEY SHORE

From Sandy Hook in the north to Island Beach State Park, the area known as the "Shore" in New Jersey offers a little bit of everything from sand

The legendary Outer Banks of Cape Hatteras, North Carolina, circa 1975.

beaches to rugged jetties. There are no rocks except for the jetties that provide excellent fishing platforms for those wearing cleated shoes to cope with the slippery surfaces. Anglers can also cast from dry rocks at the mouths of Barnegat, Manasquan, and Shark River inlets. There are probably more surfcasters here than anywhere else in the world due to the very large local population plus the proximity to both the New York and Philadelphia metropolitan areas. Beach buggies can use Island Beach year-round, and are allowed on beaches along the Ocean County coast with permits from each municipality, after the bathing season. However, Sandy Hook is strictly for walk-ons as is all of Monmouth County just below the park. Striped bass and bluefish are caught throughout the area from spring through fall, and little tunny are probably more popular among surfcasters here than anywhere else when they arrive in late summer and early fall. Bonito and Spanish mackerel are encountered occasionally. Fluke are a popular target from both beaches and jetties as are kingfish. Croakers arrive during early fall some years, though this is the northern end of their range.

Long Beach Island, which runs from the south side of Barnegat Inlet to Beach Haven Inlet, is also famed for its surfcasting, especially during the six-week surf-fishing tournament held each fall. The largest striped bass and bluefish are almost invariably beached by anglers using cut bunker or bunker heads for bait.

Ironically, the IGFA world record striped bass was caught south of there from an area not on the list of great surfcasting areas. Al McReynolds was casting from an Atlantic City jetty during a northeast storm on September 21, 1982, when he hooked his 78-pounder.

MONTAUK, LONG ISLAND, NEW YORK

The eastern end of Long Island is best-known for its rocky shoreline around Montauk Point itself, but there's also good fishing along sand beaches on the ocean side to the west as well as on the northern (Block Island Sound) side where Shagwong Point is famed for its night fishing in north winds that concentrate the bait along the shore. Montauk Point, below the lighthouse, can be a mob scene on the rocks, but there's also good wading on North Bar and lots of room on the pebble beach just to the west at Turtle Cove. Anglers can park in the large lot at the Point to access those areas on foot. The most dedicated wear wetsuits and swim out to rocks well off the beach in order to cast into prime striper territory. Striped bass and bluefish are featured, and little tunny often move into Turtle Cove during early fall. Crazy Alberto Knie lives in this area and established his reputation as one of the world's greatest surfcasters among Montauk's rocks.

RHODE ISLAND

Though it's the smallest state, Rhode Island has lots of rocky coastline and provides great shore fishing for striped bass as well as bluefish and little tunny for lure fishermen; plus tautog for those fishing crab-baits on bottom in the rocks. The breachways running from saltwater "ponds" into Block Island Sound concentrate bait and predators, and are among the finest, most easily accessible shore fishing areas in the world—just a short walk from parking lots. During the years I was covering New England for Garcia Fishing Tackle, I rarely passed up the opportunity to spend a few hours night fishing at Charlestown Breachway on the outgoing current beginning about three hours after high tide.

BLOCK ISLAND

The ferry ride from the mainland over to Rhode Island's summer resort at sea is well worth the effort for surfcasters, especially in the fall. Some of the largest surf stripers ever have been hooked here on both lures and eels, and this may be the best bet for those seeking a trophy 50-pound striper. Most of the fishing is in rocky areas, but Sandy Point is an exception. Anglers wading there must exercise great caution due to the powerful currents and waves that can easily sweep them off their feet.

THE MASSACHUSETTS ISLANDS

Martha's Vineyard is easily accessible by ferry from Woods Hole, and provides a complete range of striped bass fishing opportunities around its shorelines. With such a variety of conditions, ranging from rocks to pond openings, any type of tackle can be utilized. Casting for little tunny and bonito is also very productive during late summer. The annual Striped Bass and Bluefish Derby from mid-September to mid-October attracts thousands of surfcasters who fish day and night for prizes, but more for the glory.

Nantucket is also a ferry destination. Not generally as crowded as Martha's Vineyard, it offers great surf fishing for jumbo bluefish in the summer plus stripers in the spring and fall. Great Point, on the northeast corner, features currents and waves colliding from various directions, and presents a real challenge for the surfcaster.

Cuttyhunk is the cradle of shore fishing for big stripers. This tiny island (two miles long and a half-mile wide), the westernmost of the Elizabeth Islands, is accessed by ferry from New Bedford. The Cuttyhunk Fishing Club was established in 1864 by New York tycoons, and soon was playing host to such distinguished guests as Presidents Grover Cleveland, Teddy Roosevelt, and William Howard Taft. Stands were built over the rocks for the anglers to fish from, and guides chummed stripers in while the fishermen often baited with lobster tails. It was here that Charles B. Church caught his 73-pound striper on August 17, 1913, a bass that remained the goal of every striper fisherman until Capt. Bob Rocchetta boated his 76-pounder off Montauk on July 17, 1981. The old millionaires' club is now a bed-and-breakfast serving surfcasters who fish directly from the rocks that now show few traces of the old casting platforms.

OUTER CAPE COD, MASSACHUSETTS

The stretch of the Outer Cape from Monomoy to Race Point at Provincetown may be the most productive surf for trophy striped bass on sand beaches anywhere. That especially applies to Nauset, where the most incredible run of monster stripers occurred in 1981. Steve Petri, Jr., from Long Island, beached a 69-pounder there on August 24, and returned on November 2 for a 66-pounder, but was upstaged by Tony Stezko, who topped his many 50- and 60-pounders with a 73-pounder on November 2, which remains the unofficial record from the beach. Stezko, a print shop owner, artist, and surf fishing guide in Orleans, generally casts eels and plugs, but caught his giant striper on a black fly rigged on a dropper loop as a teaser. Monomoy used to be a peninsula, but was cut into two islands by storms. Surfcasters access Monomoy by boat, and the flats off the islands have become a favorite of wading fly-fishermen who sight-cast to stripers swimming in clear waters.

A Selection of Fishing Knots

There is a multitude of knots that anglers have used with success over the years. But the simpler the rig and the fewer knots you have to learn, the better off you'll be. Learn a few reliable knots well, when you have to rig in a hurry—or in the dark, or in a storm—you'll have less confusion and you'll get back to the fishing that much sooner.

LINE TO HOOK

Improved Clinch Knot

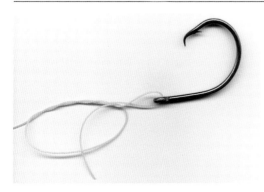

Improved clinch knot. Form the knot loosely to start.

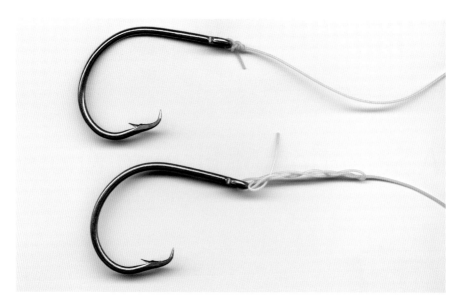

Snug the knot to assure it is formed, bottom, then snug it down by pulling on the running line, top. To maximize knot strength increase the number of turns as the line test decreases.

Trilene Knot

Trilene knot, a variation of the improved clinch knot that uses two turns through the eye of the hook. The additional turn is essential when knotting braided line directly to the hook, to prevent the knot slipping.

Loop Knot

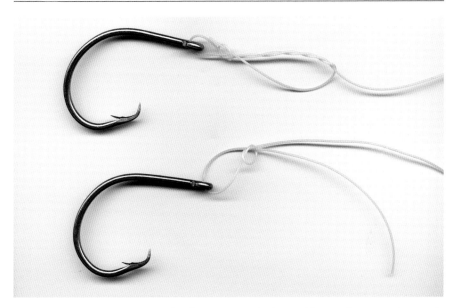

Loop knot allows the hook to swing free because the loop will not collapse on the eye. As illustrated in the lower image, this knot starts with an overhand knot before threading through the eye of the hook. To maximize knot strength increase the number of turns as the line test decreases.

LINE-TO-LINE KNOTS

Albright Knot

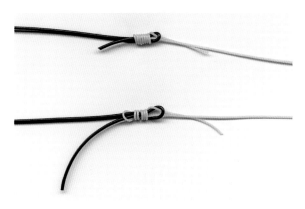

The Albright knot is useful for attaching a monofilament leader [the light-colored line in the illustration] to the end of the heavier running line [the dark colored line in the illustration].

Surgeons Knot

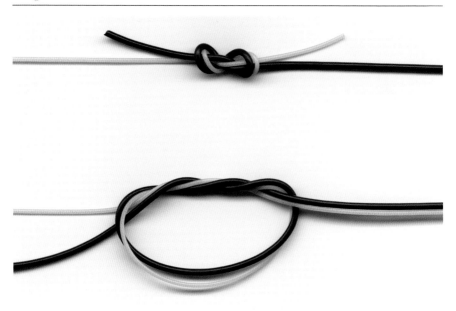

The surgeon's knot is often used to connect two dissimilar diameters of monofilament together. Make at least two turns, but no greater than 3 turns when tying this knot. When tightening this knot be sure to tighten both strands at the same time.

Blood Knot

The blood knot is often used to connect two strands of monofilament where the diameters are relatively similar.

MONO-TO-BRAIDED LINE

Braided line, super-lines, and all gel-spun polymers are notoriously strong for their diameter, but the material is also slippery, and requires that knots be carefully chosen, especially when joining it to monofilament lines which have different knotting characteristics.

Reverse Albright Knot

The reverse Albright knot is recommended to connect braided line [e.g., PowerPro] to a monofilament leader. To maximize knot strength increase the number of turns of braided line [light-colored line in the illustration].

Uni-Knot

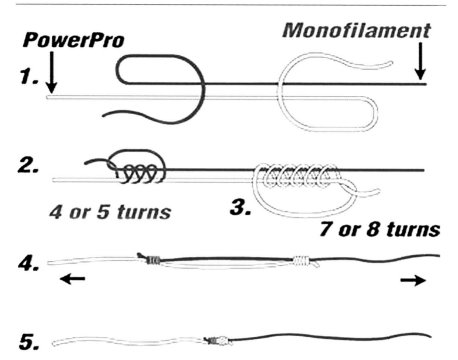

The Uni-Knot is another effective way to join braided lines, such as PowerPro, Spectra, and other gel-spun polymer lines to monofilament. To properly form the finished knot, tighten one side at a time, then draw the two sides together. (PowerPro photo)

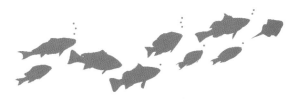

Index

O